MANY VOICES

Multilateral Negotiations
in the World Arena

Titles in This Series

Case Studies in International Affairs
Series Editor: Martin Staniland, University of Pittsburgh

The case-study approach to teaching and learning is on the rise in foreign policy and international studies classrooms. Westview Press is pleased to promote this trend by publishing a series of casebooks for a variety of college courses.

Innovative educators are using case studies to:

- Develop critical thinking skills
- Engage students in decisionmaking and role playing
- Transform lecture courses into interactive courses
- Encourage students to apply theoretical concepts using practical experience and knowledge
- Exercise skills in negotiation, management, and leadership

Each book will include theoretical and historical background material, four to eight case studies from all regions of the world, material introducing and connecting the cases, and discussion questions. Teaching notes will be provided to adopting professors, and to encourage the use of several different books and themes within a single class, the casebooks will be short, inexpensive paperbacks of approximately 150 pages.

The individual case studies making up the heart of each volume were developed in conjunction with seven institutions—University of Pittsburgh, Harvard University, Georgetown University, Columbia University, Johns Hopkins University, University of Southern California, and the International Peace Academy—under the auspices of The Pew Charitable Trusts. From over 140 case studies developed by leading scholars, the editors have selected those studies that thematically and substantively offer the best classroom examples for each topic in the series.

MANY VOICES
Multilateral Negotiations in the World Arena

edited by
ABIODUN WILLIAMS
Georgetown University

Westview Press
BOULDER ■ SAN FRANCISCO ■ OXFORD

Case Studies in International Affairs

This volume, as compiled, copyright © 1992 by Westview Press, Inc. The following case studies have been edited and are reprinted here with permission: "The Geneva Conference of 1954: Indochina" by David S. Painter and Sally G. Irvine (Pew case study no. 414) copyright © by The Pew Charitable Trusts; "NATO Negotiations on the Intermediate Range Nuclear Forces, 1977–1979" by Don R. Drenth (Pew case study no. 305) copyright © by The Pew Charitable Trusts; "The United States at UNCTAD 1" by Carol Lancaster (Pew case study no. 108) copyright © by The Pew Charitable Trusts; "The Negotiations Leading to the 1987 Montreal Protocol on Substances That Deplete the Ozone Layer" by Allan E. Goodman (Pew case study no. 447) copyright © by The Pew Charitable Trusts; "Negotiating a Minerals Regime for Antarctica" by William Westermeyer and Christopher Joyner (Pew case study no. 134) copyright © by The Pew Charitable Trusts; "International Negotiations on the Code of Conduct for Transnational Corporations" by Thomas G. Weiss and Donald Lu (Pew case study no. 202) copyright © by The Pew Charitable Trusts.

Published in 1992 in the United States of America by Westview Press, Inc., 5500 Central Avenue, Boulder, Colorado 80301-2847, and in the United Kingdom by Westview Press, 36 Lonsdale Road, Summertown, Oxford OX2 7EW

Library of Congress Cataloging-in-Publication Data
Many Voices : Multilateral Negotiations in the World Arena /
    edited by Abiodun Williams
        p. cm. — (Case studies in international affairs)
    Includes bibliographical references.
    ISBN 0-8133-1284-1 — ISBN 0-8133-1285-X (pbk.)
    1. Diplomatic negotiations in international disputes.
2. International relations. I. Williams, Abiodun, 1961–   .
II. Series.
JX4473.M36   1992
341.3—dc20   92-12535
                                                                                  CIP

Printed and bound in the United States of America

The paper used in this publication meets the requirements
of the American National Standard for Permanence of Paper
for Printed Library Materials Z39.48-1984.

10   9   8   7   6   5   4   3   2   1

To my mother

CONTENTS

FOREWORD

The Westview series Case Studies in International Affairs stems from a major project of The Pew Charitable Trusts entitled "The Pew Diplomatic Initiative." Launched in 1985, this project has sought to improve the teaching and practice of negotiation through adoption of the case method of teaching, principally in professional schools of international affairs in the United States.

By 1989, authors associated with the seven institutions involved in the Diplomatic Initiative had written over 140 case studies in international negotiation for classroom use.[1]   In considering a second phase of the program, The Pew Charitable Trusts determined that its emphasis should shift from writing cases to encouraging their adoption in courses taught through the case method.

One aspect of this phase has been the establishment of a clearinghouse at the Graduate School of Public and International Affairs, University of Pittsburgh, to distribute and promote the cases.   During the first two years of the clearinghouse's operation, it quickly became clear that a sizeable market for the case studies (and a considerable interest in case-method teaching) existed in the larger community of university and college undergraduate instruction.   By October 1990, over 15,000 single copies of cases had been sold, and the circle of customers had widened to include instructors in such countries as India, Bulgaria, and the Soviet Union.

It also became clear that, although a classroom use for individual cases would always exist, there was instructional potential in sets of cases selected to illustrate particular issues in negotiation as well as negotiations over particular policy matters.   Hence the Westview series, which offers students and instructors the opportunity to examine and discuss specific themes, including themes (such as foreign policymaking) that fall outside of the ambit of international negotiation.   Each volume presents a selection of cases, some short, others long, some essentially unchanged, others extensively edited or rewritten. Each volume also contains an introductory chapter, identifying the characteristic features and dilemmas of the kind of negotiation or issue exemplified by the cases. Each volume contains questions for discussion and suggestions for simulation and further reading.

Case-method teaching typically involves two elements. The first (and essential) element is careful reading of a case document by students. The second is one or more classroom sessions in which an instructor, using sustained Socratic questioning, tries to get students to explore the meaning of events that are described, but deliberately not interpreted or explained, in the case document.

Like all teaching, case-method teaching depends on a contract, however implicit. The contract here is framed by two norms: the first is that the material within the case provides a common stock of evidence and an obligatory point of reference. If this norm is broken by the introduction of extraneous or privileged information, the case will cease to serve as a common focus, the assumption of equal information (however artificial and fictitious it may be) will break down, and some students will feel discouraged from participating.

The second norm is one of judgmental equality—that, for purposes of the discussion, the instructor willingly suspends his or her authority for the sake of encouraging students to develop and express their own interpretations of events. Although the instructor may (indeed, should) organize discussions so as to lead students into specific questions, he or she will undermine the exploratory and interactive character of the discussions if students have the impression that they are required to discover "the right answers." This does not mean that instructors have to say (much less to believe) that they have no opinions or that one person's opinion is as good as another's. It simply means that they should be prepared to retreat, temporarily, to the roles of agenda-setter and discussion leader, rather than assuming those of decisionmaker and interpreter.

Although obviously there are some important premises regarding educational philosophy and psychology underpinning belief in case-method teaching, the case for instructors holding back is essentially pragmatic—that discussion is a good educational vehicle and that students will only climb onto it if they are allowed to share in the driving.

Case-method teaching is, then, a tool, supplementing the conventional tools of exposition. Cases can be used to follow up lectures; they can (as this series implies) be used comparatively; they can be used for discussion or for simulation. They can be used with or without accompanying writing assignments. They can be used to illustrate theoretical concepts (such as power) or to require students to enter into the agonies of political choice ("What would you have done if you were President Carter?"). But what they invariably do is to enable—and to force—students to take responsibility for their own political and academic education. The faint burning smell of hard thinking hangs in the air after a good case discussion has taken place. Surely anything that produces that smell should be welcome.

Martin Staniland
Series Editor

NOTES

1. The institutions concerned were the School of International Relations, University of Southern California; the School of International and Public Affairs, Columbia University; the Edmund A. Walsh School of Foreign Service, Georgetown University; the John F. Kennedy School of Government, Harvard University; the International Peace Academy (of the United Nations); the Paul H. Nitze School of Advanced International Studies, Johns Hopkins University; and the Graduate School of Public and International Affairs, University of Pittsburgh.

ACKNOWLEDGMENTS

I have benefited greatly from the the help I received from a number of people while I was preparing this manuscript. I am grateful to my colleague Allan E. Goodman for suggesting that I pursue this project and for his support. A Pew Faculty Fellowship made it possible for me to spend time at Harvard's John F. Kennedy School of Government where I studied the use of cases in teaching international relations. I appreciate the patience, advice, and assistance of Martin Staniland, the series editor of Case Studies in International Affairs, and Jennifer Knerr of Westview Press. My research assistant, Chelsea Cochrane, gave indispensable help by typing a large portion of the manuscript.

Finally, I owe an enormous debt of gratitude to my sister Valerie for her thoughtful editorial suggestions, good humor—and more.

Abiodun Williams

1

INTRODUCTION

Interest in the study of diplomacy and negotiation is not a new phenomenon. Since the early eighteenth century, when François de Callieres published his classic, *On the Manner of Negotiating with Princes*, much ink has been spilt on the subject.[1] A recently published bibliography on negotiations is an ample volume of 417 pages.[2] The study of negotiation continues to be a growth industry, as scholars and practitioners of all stripes attempt to make sense—some with more success than others—of its complex and often opaque nature. Our understanding of the subject has been greatly enhanced by the literature that has been published during the past three decades. Although many of the contributions have come from political scientists, they by no means have cornered the market. Economists, sociologists, psychologists, historians, and lawyers have illuminated this territory, and political scientists themselves have often drawn on the insights of other disciplines.

CONTENDING APPROACHES

There are a number of contending analytical approaches to negotiation. Influenced by the tradition of economics, some students of negotiation view it in terms of a "game," with its own set of "players" and "rules." A deductive method of analysis is usually employed, with a strong emphasis on bargaining strategies utilized by rational individuals.[3] Many other studies focus on giving advice on how to negotiate successfully. In contrast to game theorists, authors of these practical guides favor the inductive method, and a wide array of case studies inform their analyses. Underlying the didactic approach is the belief that negotiation can be taught through the mastery of certain methods and principles. Advocates of that approach reject the view that the tricks of the trade can only be learned by a process of professional osmosis. Whether negotiation is viewed as a "zero-sum game" or as a "win-win" enterprise, the advice proferred runs the gamut from how to prepare for negotiations to strategies to be used during the process and pitfalls to be avoided.[4] A third sociopsychological approach focuses on the character of individual negotiators and the impact of their personalities, worldviews, and philosophies on the conduct of negotiations.[5] A closely related method of analysis, but much broader in scope, can be characterized as the cultural-national perspective. The emphasis here is on, not individual attributes or traits, but the influence of culture and national background on different negotiating styles.[6]

Although there has been a plethora of studies on negotiation generally, and on bilateral negotiations in particular, relatively few have concentrated on multilateral negotiation. This, to some degree, is a reflection of the difficulty involved in having to take into account the many relevant variables that affect the nature, process, and outcome of multilateral negotiations. Although it is generally recognized that there are differences between bilateral and multilateral negotiation, multilateral negotiation is often regarded as merely an enlarged version of what occurs bilaterally. Its distinctive elements and the skills required for success have seldom been articulated. The search continues for the important but elusive comprehensive analytical framework that can be used to further our understanding of this cardinal component of modern international relations.

In attempting a typology of multilateral negotiations, one is immediately confronted with definitional problems. It is customary to define a multilateral negotiation as a negotiation involving more than two participants. Definitions in this context are not necessarily right or wrong, but some are more useful than others. This definition, which is both minimalist and maximalist, is not particularly helpful, as it obscures the fact that there can be significant differences, for example, between a negotiation having five participants and one with fifty. Midgaard and Underdal distinguish three kinds of multilateral negotiations on the basis of the number of participants. *Small* multilateral negotiations they define as having fewer than seven parties, *intermediate* ones have between seven and twenty, and *large* multilateral negotiations have over twenty.[7] This classification is not particularly helpful either because the smallest multilateral negotiations today often have around twenty parties. It is useful to consider *small* multilateral negotiations as having up to twenty parties, *medium-sized* ones as having between twenty and sixty, and *large* ones as those with over sixty participants.[8]

ACTORS

Since the Treaty of Westphalia in 1648 laid the foundation of the modern international system, sovereign states have been the primary actors in the international system. Traditionally, the actors who have participated in multilateral negotiations have been *states* and their governmental representatives. One of the most significant developments since the end of World War II is the dramatic increase in the number of independent states. In 1945, when the United Nations was founded, the organization had only 51 members, but nearly 180 states have joined the world body. This quantitative change in the nature of the international system has had a profound impact on world politics and, in particular, has led to greater complexity in the conduct of multilateral negotiations. Although the sovereign equality of states is a fundamental principle of the international system, there are vast disparities between different states in terms of their military strength, economic resources, and diplomatic leverage. Similar or unequal capabilities between states may result in symmetrical or asymmetrical negotiations.

Although states are still the primary participants in multilateral negotiations, an increasing number of *nonstate actors*, such as international organizations (e.g., the United Nations—UN), regional organizations (e.g., the European Economic Community—EEC), nongovernmental organizations (e.g., the International Olympic Committee), and multinational corporations (MNCs; e.g., IBM), are now involved in multilateral negotiations.[9] The number of nonstate actors has grown as substantially as that of states in the post-World War II period. For example, in 1940 there were about 500 nongovernmental organizations, but by the end of the 1980s this number had increased to over 4,000. Some nonstate actors, such as multinational corporations, have not only mushroomed numerically but have increased the scope of their influence in the global economy as well.

Many contemporary multilateral negotiations are conducted under the auspices of an *international organization*, especially the United Nations. The United Nations has sponsored negotiations dealing with a vast array of security, economic, environmental, and social issues. The General Assembly, the only organ in which all member states are represented, has played a crucial role in negotiating different multilateral treaties, such as the Law of the Sea Treaty and the Genocide Convention, which prohibits acts aimed at eliminating a national, ethnic, racial, or religious group. The choice of a forum in which negotiations take place is a crucial one that can send certain signals to the parties, affect the outcome, and set a precedent for the future. The genesis of the first United Nations Conference on Trade and Development (UNCTAD), which was held in 1964, can be traced to the fact that less developed countries (LDCs) were disenchanted with certain international economic institutions, especially the General Agreement on Tariffs and Trade (GATT), which they felt were not adequately addressing their developmental concerns. They favored a separate forum under the aegis of the United Nations, which they felt would be a more hospitable environment in which to discuss matters of trade and development.

ISSUES

Multilateral negotiations have historically dealt with what were considered to be issues of "high politics," peace, and security. The Congress of Vienna in 1815, the first modern multilateral conference, was convoked in order to lay the foundations of a new European order in the wake of the ravages of the Napoleonic wars. Republics were absorbed, several monarchies were reinstated, and a nineteenth-century equivalent of the Holy Roman Empire was created. Subsequent multilateral conferences in the nineteenth century, such as the Berlin Congress of 1884-1885, in which the African continent was divided among the major European powers, continued this tradition. Nowadays, however, multilateral negotiations cover a broad range of issues: security, economics, trade and finance, environment, natural resources, human rights, science and technology. This reflects the growing complexity of world affairs and the concomitant increase in the number of issues on the international diplomatic agenda. Human rights, social issues, and problems with global resource management are becoming as important as, if not more important than, concerns with war and peace.

The Role of Coalitions

A distinguishing feature of multilateral negotiations is the frequent formation of blocs, groups, or coalitions among the various participants, which later may become permanent or institutionalized.[10] Many of these blocs are deliberate creations of their members on the basis of shared characteristics or common interests. There are regional alliances, whose organizing principle is geography, such as the traditional regional groups in the United Nations: the African Group, the Asian Group, the Latin American Group, and the Western European and Others Group; political coalitions (e.g., the Arab League, Commonwealth, Nonaligned); blocs based on intergovernmental economic treaties (e.g., Benelux, Organization for Economic Cooperation and Development [OECD], and African, Caribbean, and Pacific countries associated with the European Community [ACP]); and groups that share other attributes such as a similar level of economic development (e.g., the Group of 77).

In many North-South negotiations, blocs play an important role in the process. In UNCTAD, the Group of 77 (now composed of some 120 countries) represents the developing countries; Group B is made up of the industrialized countries that are members of the OECD; and Group D is composed of the former Socialist countries of Eastern Europe, but the latter have played a limited role in UNCTAD negotiations. Although these groups endeavor to present a united front during negotiations, they are not monolithic entities. The members of the Group of 77 (G-77) include oil-producing countries such as Nigeria and Venezuela, newly industrializing countries such as South Korea and Brazil, and much poorer states such as Chad. Differences in economic systems and levels of economic performance also exist among members of Group B, although not to the same degree as in the Group of 77.

Before and during negotiations, groups sometimes form spontaneously to deal with particular problems or in response to a crisis. The Coastal States Group, composed of about seventy-six coastal countries, was established a year before the start of the Third United Nations Conference on the Law of the Sea (1973-1982) to secure extended coastal-state jurisdiction, especially with regard to the exclusive economic zone. During the concluding period of the eleventh session of the conference, the Group of 12, which earned the sobriquet the "Good Samaritans," was formed in order to fashion a consensus text and to prevent a divisive vote.[11]

As Johan Kaufmann demonstrated, groups perform a multiplicity of functions. They exchange information on all or part of the agenda of a conference either in advance or during the negotiations; develop common general positions on key agenda items without committing themselves to voting in a particular way; develop unified positions on some agenda items with definite voting commitments; agree on common candidates from the group or on supporting candidates from other groups; select a common spokesperson and reach agreement on the statement to be delivered; and take joint action in favor of or against a proposal.[12] But coalitions are a mixed blessing. They can make the negotiating environment less complex and enhance the efficient conduct of negotiations. However, there is always the possibility of an attack of "coalitionitis," as blocs may become rigid and inflexible, stumbling blocks to success. Negotiating blocs are not necessarily more amenable to reason and moderation than individual states. In order not to become hostage to the negative tendencies of coalitions, the Commission on Transnational Corporations adopted an innovative procedure during the preliminary stages of the negotiations on a code of conduct. It departed from the usual practice of having the various regional groups in the United Nations submit their respective draft proposals that then formed the bases of often prolonged, and sometimes acrimonious, debates. Instead, its working group drafted an outline of the code, and the chairman submitted additional proposals known as "formulations." Negotiations and the subsequent drafting of the text were based on the outline and formulations.

Because multilateral negotiations usually include numerous parties, they are potentially unwieldy and thus must contend with the problems that result from their size and number. There are a greater number of objectives to be reconciled, many different cultural and political attitudes to be accommodated, more voices to be heard, and more feathers to become ruffled. The formation of blocs is one mechanism that is frequently employed to cope with difficulties that stem from size, but it is not the only one. Like many national legislatures and assemblies, the setting up of committees or working groups is an important element in multilateral negotiations. For example, committees may be created to deal with a particular problem or to draft the text of a treaty.

Rules of Procedure

Another strategy to cope with the challenges of size is the adoption of formal rules of procedure, which provide the framework within which negotiations are conducted. Generally, rules of procedure include the following: the number and rank of the parties; the languages to be used; the rights of the participants; the length and frequency of the sessions; and the method of decisionmaking. Procedural arrangements can influence the outcome of negotiations, and shrewd negotiators can use them to advantage. As in bilateral negotiations, the order of items on the agenda is crucial, as this can also have an effect on the outcome. In the multilateral setting, the agenda order takes on added significance, for it is more difficult to change earlier decisions because of the number of participants.

If there is one individual who can do the most to further the success of a negotiation, it is the chairperson. He or she must have the capacity to reconcile divergent and sometimes conflicting views. Like a skillful conductor, the chairperson has to give harmony to discordant voices, and like a referee he or she must be decisive without being overweening. Philip C. Jessup, who served on the International Court of Justice, gave the following description of the special talents required for success:

> The wise and experienced chairman usually can "feel" the temper of the meeting and will know when to assert his authority firmly and when to allow a procedural discussion to continue until a solution emerges. He should be able to detect the difference between a sincere argument about the procedure which the delegate believes will lead to the most satisfactory disposition of the business before the meeting, and the tactics of obstruction or the stubborn insistence upon a point of view which the delegate will not abandon but which the group clearly will not accept. The more the chairman allows himself to be drawn into controversy, the less does he act in a judicial capacity and the less successful he is apt to be in discharging his duties.[13]

The chairperson can be a member of one of the delegations but after election cannot vote. On other occasions, if negotiations are being held under the auspices of an international organization, the chairperson is often the secretary-general. During GATT negotiations, individual committees are chaired by officials of its secretariat.

THE PROCESS: A FRAMEWORK

Multilateral negotiations vary not only in the kind and number of parties involved and the issues that are the subject of negotiations but also in the form and process of the actual negotiations themselves. Nevertheless, it is possible to identify certain phases in the negotiation process that are characteristic of many multinational negotiations. All six cases in this volume are structured to illustrate three distinct negotiating phases.

Deciding to Negotiate

International relations have become very complex during the last forty-five years, with a plethora of issues and problems that demand multilateral solutions. Multilateral negotiations are essential in solving these problems and in dealing with unpredictability and change in the international system. Although countries remain concerned about the enduring problems of security and defense, other issues relating to the environment, health, trade and finance, and technology are gaining increasing importance in world politics. As the cases in this volume demonstrate, parties may enter negotiations in order to bring an end to a military conflict (as illustrated in Chapter 2, "Negotiating a Settlement in Indochina"); to further their security interests (as discussed in Chapter 3, "Negotiating NATO's Deployment of Intermediate Nuclear Forces"); to address trade and development issues (as covered in Chapter 4, "Negotiations at UNCTAD I"); to deal with environmental dangers (as exemplified in Chapter 5, "Negotiating the Montreal Ozone Protocol"); to resolve competing claims over natural resources (as discussed in Chapter 6, "Negotiating a Minerals Regime for Antarctica"); or to deal with the activities of certain actors in the international system (the subject of Chapter 7, "Negotiating the Code of Conduct for Transnational Corporations").

Reaching an Agreement

The difficulties associated with bilateral negotiations are often compounded in multilateral negotiations, involving as they do a greater number of parties with varied interests, goals, and objectives, as well as different national, cultural, and linguistic backgrounds. Negotiators have to take into account not only the positions of their respective governments and domestic interest groups but also those of the regional bloc or coalition to which their country belongs. The ability to work within a coalition and with other coalitions is an important element in the process. The skillful negotiator has to grapple with a number of key questions, including: When and on what matters should I compromise? Will such compromises be reciprocated? What use should be made of formal conference sessions?

Endgame

During many multilateral negotiations, the final elements of a treaty or agreement are usually hammered out under significant time pressure and in the last stage of the process. The setting of deadlines and the awareness that time is limited often create a certain momentum that leads the different parties to shift their positions and compromise. It is during this phase of negotiations that final decisions are usually reached either by consensus or by voting.

NOTES

1. See François de Callieres, *On the Manner of Negotiating with Princes* (Notre Dame: University of Notre Dame Press, 1963). Another classic on diplomatic negotiation is Harold Nicolson, *Diplomacy* (Washington, D.C.: Institute for the Study of Diplomacy, 1989). Another insightful study is Fred C. Ikle, *How Nations Negotiate* (New York: Harper and Row, 1964).

2. Amos Lakos, *International Negotiations: A Bibliography* (Boulder: Westview Press, 1989).

3. For a good introduction to this approach by one of its preeminent exponents, see Thomas Schelling, *The Strategy of Conflict* (New York: Oxford University Press, 1963). Also useful is Glenn Snyder and Paul Diesing, *Conflict Among Nations: Bargaining and Decision-Making in International Crises* (Princeton: Princeton University Press, 1977).

4. Some examples of this genre are Roger Fisher and William Ury, *Getting to Yes: Negotiating Agreement Without Giving In* (Boston: Houghton Mifflin, 1981); and I. William Zartman and Maureen Berman, *The Practical Negotiator* (New Haven: Yale University Press, 1982).

5. See for instance, Herbert C. Kelman, ed., *International Behaviour: A Socio-Psychological Analysis* (New York: Holt Rinehart and Winston, 1965).

6. See for example, Michael Blaker, *Japanese Negotiating Style* (New York: Columbia University Press, 1977).

7. Knut Midgaard and Arild Underdal, "Multiparty Conferences," in Daniel Druckman, ed., *Negotiations: Social-Psychological Perspectives* (Beverly Hills: Sage Publications, 1977), 329-345.

8. Johan Kaufmann, *Conference Diplomacy: An Introductory Analysis*, 2d rev. ed. (Dordrecht: Martinus Nijoff, 1988), 47.

9. A good survey of the role and influence of nonstate actors in international relations is Phillip Taylor, *Nonstate Actors in International Politics: From Transregional to Substate Organizations* (Boulder: Westview Press, 1984).

10. This discussion of alliances and coalitions is based on the useful volume by Kaufmann, *Conference Diplomacy*, 146-159.

11. The twelve countries were Australia, Austria, Canada, Denmark, Finland, Iceland, Ireland, New Zealand, Norway, Sweden, Switzerland, and the Netherlands. The group was created in order to propose amendments to the convention, which would taken into account some of the concerns of the United States.

12. Kaufmann, *Conference Diplomacy*, 152-154.

13. Quoted in *ibid.*, 79.

2

NEGOTIATING A
SETTLEMENT IN
INDOCHINA

The Geneva Conference of 1954, which was held to negotiate a settlement of the Indochina conflict, involved five major powers: the United States, the Soviet Union, China, France, and Great Britain. One of the major diplomatic conferences of the twentieth century, the Geneva Conference was a watershed in the history of the Indochina conflict. This case study demonstrates the advantages and limitations of summit diplomacy, and how great powers in the international system use diplomacy to reconcile divergent and conflicting national objectives. It is an example of a *small* multilateral negotiation with a limited number of participants, one that focused on issues of *peace and security*. It also highlights the difficulties in resolving conflicts that have local, regional, and international dimensions.

DECIDING TO NEGOTIATE

In April 1954, an international conference assembled in Geneva, Switzerland, to resolve the conflict in Indochina.[1] The conference originated

---

This chapter is an edited version of the case study by David S. Painter and Sally G. Irvine, The Geneva Conference of 1954: Indochina, *Pew case study no. 414.*

in a proposal by Soviet Foreign Minister Vyacheslav Molotov at the opening session of the Berlin Foreign Ministers' Meeting, in January 1954, that the conference consider (in addition to the German question and the Austrian State Treaty) the convening of a five-power conference (consisting of the People's Republic of China, the United States, Britain, France, and the Soviet Union) to "seek measures for reducing tensions in international relations." As President Dwight D. Eisenhower later noted, the United States was skeptical of the "validity of negotiations with the Soviets and Chinese Communists." Nevertheless, faced with the desire of both France and Great Britain for such a conference, the United States, citing the importance of Western unity, reluctantly agreed to a conference on Far Eastern problems.[2]

After two weeks of hard negotiations, the conferees agreed on a communique calling for a five-power conference on Korea and Indochina. Although agreeing to the inclusion of the People's Republic, the United States insisted that the communique include the statement that "neither the invitation to, nor the holding of, the . . . conference shall be deemed to imply diplomatic recognition in any case where it has not already been accorded."[3]

Indochina and the Interested Powers

Indochina. By the spring of 1954 the Front for the Independence of Vietnam, better known as the Vietminh, under the political leadership of Ho Chi Minh and the military guidance of General Vo Nguyen Giap, had been engaged for eight years in a war with the French, who had resumed their pre-World War II position as the colonial government of the three Indochinese states of Vietnam (composed of the regions Tonkin, Annam, and Cochin China), Laos, and Cambodia. In August 1945, Ho and his supporters, head-quartered in Tonkin, proclaimed the establishment of the Democratic Republic of Vietnam (DRVN). After inconclusive negotiations between the French and the Vietminh, fighting broke out in December 1946.

The DRVN was governed on the basis of the Vietminh interpretation of Marxist-Leninist and Maoist principles. In late January 1950, the Soviet Union and the People's Republic of China recognized the DRVN. By 1954, the Vietminh had extended their authority over two-thirds of Tonkin, where, outside of Hanoi, Haiphong, and a few big towns, the bulk of the countryside was in their hands. Apart from enclaves around Hue, Danang, and a few other towns, the Vietminh also held most of the coastal regions in Annam, and about half of the Mekong Delta.[4]

Meanwhile, in June 1948, the French imperial office had established a provisional national government for Vietnam, headed by Bao Dai, who had been emperor until his abdication and removal to France in 1945. The resulting State of Vietnam (SVN), headquartered in Cochin China, officially took its place as an associated state within the French Union (the association linking France and its former colonies) in early February 1950 and was formally recognized by Great Britain and the United States shortly thereafter.

Neither a popular nor an inspiring leader, Bao Dai was faced with opposition from powerful noncommunist nationalist factions as well as from the Vietminh, who refused to recognize his authority and claimed that their movement represented the genuine will of the Vietnamese people. The most notable noncommunist nationalist grouping was headed by Ngo Dinh Diem and his brother Ngo Dinh Nhu.

In 1954, both Laos and Cambodia had royal governments; both also had active resistance groups. The Pathet Lao in Laos and the Khmer Issarak (later Khmer Rouge) in Cambodia were modeled upon and assisted by the Vietminh. About half of Laos and parts of Cambodia were in the hands of the Vietminh and their allies. In October 1953, the French had signed a treaty with Laos that guaranteed Laotian independence within the French Union.

France. By the end of 1953, France had over 500,000 troops in Indochina. Only 80,000 of these were actually French, however, the rest consisting of 20,000 members of the French foreign legion, 48,000 soldiers from France's African colonies, and 369,000 Indochinese (preponderantly Vietnamese) soldiers. Because of the unpopular nature of the war, the French government refrained from sending conscripts to Indochina, and the French contingent in Indochina, though numerically small, contained 37 percent of the French army's noncommissioned officers and 26 percent of its regular officers.[5]

The large number of officers in Indochina, coupled with the high casualty rate, put severe limits on the number and quality of troops France was able to make available for European defense. In addition, France's military expenditures in Indochina, despite the fact that the United States was increasingly underwriting the cost of the war, constituted over one-third of the total French military budget, further restricting France's ability to play a major role in European defense. As their military problems in Indochina grew, the French delayed their decision regarding participation in the European Defense Community (EDC), which had been proposed as a means of providing for a West German contribution to European defense. French participation in the EDC was viewed as vital to its success.

Following the conclusion of the Korean armistice in July 1953, French political leaders talked increasingly of the possibility of a corresponding settlement in Indochina. Under pressure from critics who had begun to doubt the wisdom of continuing the war, French Prime Minister Joseph Laniel announced in November 1953 that "if an honorable settlement were in sight, on either the local or the international level, France would be happy to accept a diplomatic solution to the conflict." The Laniel government refused, however, to consider any settlement that jeopardized the integrity of the French Union.[6]

China. China had a long history of dominating Southeast Asia by manufacturing or exacerbating divisions within the Indochinese social and political communities. Vietnam and Laos, both bordering on China's southern provinces, were of critical strategic importance, especially in light of repeated U.S. threats to employ atomic weapons against Chinese territory.

The Chinese began to provide small amounts of military assistance to the DRVN in early 1950. During the summer of 1953 when fighting in Korea came to a halt, Chinese assistance began to expand significantly, though even at its flood tide in the spring of 1954 it was, according to U.S. estimates, only about one-tenth of U.S. aid to the French war effort in Indochina. The end of fighting in Korea also released Chinese combat forces for possible use in Vietnam. However, the People's Republic, since completing an agreement with India on Tibet in April 1953, had been seeking to improve its relations with the uncommitted states of Asia and Africa by emphasizing its dedication to peace in Asia and its commitment to cooperation for mutual development, as well as its continued dedication to the elimination of the remnants of colonialism and imperialism from Asia.[7]

The United States. By 1954, the United States was deeply concerned about the situation in Indochina. Although U.S. aid to France in the 1940s had indirectly supported the French war effort, the United States had refrained from providing France direct military and financial assistance for the conflict until May 1950. Between the spring of 1950 and the end of June 1954, the U.S. monetary contribution to the French war effort in Indochina totaled approximately $2.76 billion, the U.S. contribution in fiscal 1954 accounting for 78 percent of the total cost of the war to France. This aid to France constituted a significant proportion of the total U.S. foreign assistance program.[8]

On January 12, 1954, Secretary of State John Foster Dulles reiterated earlier warnings to the Chinese that any overt aggression in Indochina would have "grave consequences which might not be confined to Indochina." In early February, President Eisenhower increased the U.S. Military Assistance Advisory Group stationed in Indochina and sent additional arms to the French. After Congress raised questions about his intentions in Southeast Asia, particularly regarding the possible dispatch of U.S. troops, Eisenhower responded on February 10 that there could be "no greater tragedy for America than to get heavily involved in an all-out war in any of those regions." Under Secretary of State Walter Bedell Smith elaborated the president's remarks the following week by noting that the administration would refrain from taking any major military decisions about Indochina without prior consultation with Congress.[9]

The Soviet Union. In 1954 the Soviet Union was pursuing a policy of "peaceful coexistence," which had been adopted following the death of Joseph

Stalin in March 1953. Political leadership during 1953 and 1954 was divided between two factions: that of Georgy Malenkov, who substantially controlled the apparatus of state; and that of Nikita Khrushchev, who substantially controlled the apparatus of the Communist Party. Though the chief disagreement between these two groups centered upon economic policy, there was also considerable debate about the proper direction of Soviet foreign policy, particularly regarding the possibility of a "general war" with the West. Malenkov's faction believed that the possibility of a war with the United States was slight because of the mutually deterring effect of atomic weapons. Khrushchev and many Soviet military men, in contrast, were concerned about the apparent aggressiveness of U.S. rhetoric, if not actions, and argued that the Soviet Union needed to remain vigilant to prevent possible U.S. aggression.[10]

Although Indochina, like the rest of Southeast Asia, was an area of marginal importance to the Soviet Union, the evolving situation presented problems for Soviet leaders. If, on the one hand, the Vietminh won a major victory with Chinese support, Moscow's position as leader of world communism could be diminished. If, on the other hand, the situation in Indochina stimulated U.S. military intervention, and possibly even action against China itself, the Soviet Union might become involved either because of its treaty commitments to defend China or because the conflict could escalate into a general war.[11]

Great Britain. The British were very interested in a political settlement of the Indochina conflict. Although they had supported the reimposition of French rule in Indochina following World War II, by the spring of 1954 the British were convinced that the French position was untenable and were concerned that the conflict could easily escalate into a wider war. Moreover, the British were concerned about Malaya and wanted to keep the Communists as far away from their resource-rich colony as possible. The British were also influenced by the position of India and the other Asian Commonwealth countries in favor of a negotiated settlement. At the Berlin meeting, Foreign Secretary Anthony Eden had joined the Soviets in pushing for an international conference on Indochina.[12]

The Battle of Dienbienphu and Preconference Maneuvering

In hope of regaining the military initiative in the war, the French had adopted a new strategy in 1953, the Navarre Plan, named after General Henri Navarre, commander of French forces in Indochina. The plan called for increasing the number of Vietnamese troops and utilizing them to hold areas cleared by French Union troops, thereby freeing French Union forces to consolidate the French position in the north. General Giap's move into Laos in April 1953 disrupted these plans, however, and in November, Navarre tried to regain the initiative by concentrating his best forces at the remote northwest Tonkin village of Dienbienphu astride a major route into Laos. Navarre hoped to draw Vietminh forces into the open, where they would be vulnerable to French superior firepower and control of the air.[13]

This move proved to be a major mistake, and the French position at Dienbienphu deteriorated rapidly, as the Vietminh, with Chinese assistance, moved heavy artillery and anti-aircraft guns into the hills surrounding the French position. In March 1954, French General Paul Ely traveled to Washington to discuss increased military assistance and the possibility of U.S. military intervention in Indochina. Although the United States approved Ely's request for the loan of twenty-five additional bombers, the Eisenhower administration insisted that before it would consider military intervention several conditions would have to be met, including (1) granting of "true sovereignty" to Cambodia, Laos, and the State of Vietnam; (2) a request from those states for U.S. help, including U.S. training for their armed forces; (3) approval by the United Nations; (4) cooperation of major U.S. allies; and (5) prior congressional approval.[14]

None of these conditions was met: the French were unwilling to give up control of Indochina and had resisted taking the issue to the United Nations for fear of the possible impact on their other colonies; congressional leaders insisted on Indochinese independence and firm commitments of support from U.S. allies, particularly Britain; and the British opposed military intervention for several reasons. The British believed that air action alone would not be effective; they were concerned that military intervention would destroy any hope for a negotiated settlement; and they feared that direct military involvement might lead to a wider war in Asia, if not a third world war.[15]

Dulles outlined U.S. policy toward Indochina in an address to the Overseas Press Club on March 29. Noting that "the French Government last July declared its intention to complete [Vietnamese] independence, and negotiations to consummate that pledge are actively underway," he charged that the Communists were "attempting to prevent the orderly development of independence" and were planning "to dominate all of Southeast Asia." He stated that "that possibility should not be passively accepted, but should be met by united action."[16]

Dulles elaborated his concept of "united action" in talks with French Ambassador Henri Bonnet on April 3. What he had in mind, he explained, was a regional military alliance of the United States, Great Britain, France, Australia, New Zealand, Thailand, the Philippines, and the Associated States of Indochina to defend the region against communism. The following day, President Eisenhower wrote British Prime Minster Winston Churchill that the United States had concluded that "there is no negotiated solution of the

Indochina problem which in its essence would not be either a face-saving device to cover a French surrender or a face-saving device to cover a Communist retirement." Because the first alternative was "too serious in its broad strategic implications" to be acceptable, Eisenhower urged the British to cooperate in establishment of a "coalition composed of nations which have a vital concern in the checking of Communist expansion in the area." Eisenhower stressed "that the coalition must be strong and it must be willing to join the fight if necessary." The United States also contacted the other potential members.[17]

Eisenhower further clarified the U.S. position in an April 7 press conference. Asked to comment on "the strategic importance of Indochina to the free world," he explained:

> First of all, you have the specific value of a locality in its production of materials that the world needs.
>
> Then you have the possibility that many human beings pass under a dictatorship that is inimical to the free world.
>
> Finally, you have broader considerations that might follow what you would call the "falling domino" principle. You have a row of dominoes set up, you knock over the first one, and what will happen to the last one is the certainty that it will go over very quickly. So you could have a beginning of a disintegration that would have the most profound influences.[18]

Dulles met with British and French leaders in London and Paris in mid-April to discuss united action. Although both allies expressed interest in the concept, both were reluctant to take any action that might compromise the chances of achieving a negotiated settlement at Geneva.[19]

The Soviet Union charged that Dulles was trying to poison the atmosphere for the Geneva Conference and called U.S. plans for a regional military alliance an attempt to suppress "the national liberation movement of Asian peoples" in order to preserve Western colonial domination of Asia. The Soviets also charged that the United States was planning to establish a bridge-head in Indochina from which it could attack the People's Republic of China.[20]

Meanwhile, the French colonial office and representatives of the State of Vietnam had reopened long-standing negotiations for Vietnamese independence. Throughout March and April, Prince Bu Loc, the Vietnamese foreign minister, insisted upon an unequivocal grant of independence, to be followed by Vietnamese entrance into the French Union. The French argued that guarantees of a bond with the French Union had to precede any relinquishment of French control. On April 25, after meeting with Dulles in

Paris, Bao Dai endorsed the U.S. proposal for a regional collective security organization and announced that neither he nor the government of the State of Vietnam would consider itself bound "by decisions which run counter to the independence and unity of their country at the same time that they violate a people's rights and offer to reward aggression." Three days later, the French and the Bao Dai government released a statement announcing their intention to conclude two treaties: the first, recognizing "the total independence of Viet Nam and her full and entire sovereignty"; the second, establishing "a Franco-Viet Nam association in the French Union founded on equality and intended to develop the cooperation between the two countries."[21]

As their position at Dienbienphu grew critical in late April, the French, though still unwilling to meet U.S. political conditions, renewed their request for direct U.S. military involvement. Despite considerable pressure from Dulles, the British continued to refuse to support either armed intervention or united action. Without commitments from both Britain and France, the United States declined to act unilaterally. On May 7, the French garrison at Dienbienphu surrendered.[22]

DISCUSSION QUESTIONS

1. *What was at stake in Southeast Asia for each of the parties?*
2. *What were the advantages and disadvantages of unilateral military intervention by the United States?*
3. *How could Dulles have persuaded the British to support military intervention?*
4. *What were the costs and benefits of "united action"?*

THE GENEVA CONFERENCE: OPENING REMARKS AND PROPOSALS

The first plenary session of the Indochina phase of the Geneva Conference opened on May 8. Heading the seven major delegations were Foreign Minister Georges Bidault of France, Foreign Minister Pham Van Dong of the Democratic Republic of Vietnam, Foreign Minister Nguyen Quoc Dinh of the State of Vietnam, Premier Chou En-lai of the People's Republic of China, U.S. Secretary of State John Foster Dulles, Soviet Foreign Minister Vyacheslav Molotov, and British Foreign Secretary Anthony Eden.

Bidault, the first delegate recognized, offered the following proposal for a settlement:

① France

I. Viet-Nam
1. Regroupment of regular units in regrouping zones to be determined by the Conference on proposal of the High Commands.
2. Disarmament of all elements which belong neither to the army nor to the police forces.
3. Immediate liberation of prisoners of war and civil internees.
4. Control of the execution of these clauses by international commissions.
5. Cessation of hostilities upon signature of the agreement.

The regroupment of forces and the disarmament provided above will commence no later than X days after the signing of the agreement.

II. Cambodia and Laos
1. Evacuation of all regular and irregular Viet Minh forces which have invaded the country.

2., 3. & 4. [same as above]

III.
The guarantee of the agreements is assured by the member States of the Geneva Conference. Any violation will entail an immediate consultation between these States in order to take the appropriate measures individually or collectively.[23]

② DRVN

Pham Van Dong, the head of the DRVN delegation, followed with a proposal that representatives of the resistance governments of the Pathet Lao and the Khmer Issarak be seated at the conference; this proposal was endorsed by Molotov and Chou En-lai. U.S. representative Bedell Smith, who had replaced Dulles as head of the delegation, rejected the DRVN proposal, as did the heads of the Cambodian and Laotian delegations, who considered these two groups bandits subject to manipulation by foreign powers.[24] At the second plenary session, on May 10, Pham Van Dong presented his government's proposals:

1. Recognition by France of the sovereignty and independence of Viet-Nam over the whole of the territory of Viet-Nam, as well as the sovereignty and independence of Khmer and Pathet Lao [Cambodia and Laos].
2. Conclusion of an agreement on the withdrawal of all foreign troops from the territories of Viet-Nam, Khmer, and Pathet Lao within a time period which must be fixed by concert among the

belligerent parties. Before the withdrawal of troops, it is necessary to agree on the subject of stationing of French troops in Viet-Nam, with particular attention to limiting the number of their stationing points as much as possible. It is clearly understood that the French troops are to refrain from interfering in the affairs of the local administration in the areas of their stationing.

3. Organization of free, general elections in Viet-Nam, in Khmer and Pathet Lao in order to form a single Government in each country. Convening of consultative conferences composed of representatives of the Governments of the two parties respectively in Viet-Nam, in Khmer, and in Pathet Lao in order to prepare and organize the free elections. These consultative conferences will take all measures to guarantee the free activity of patriotic parties, groups, and social organizations. No foreign intervention will be allowed. Local commissions will be formed to control the preparation and the organization of elections. Pending the formation of single governments in each of the Indochinese countries and after an agreement is reached conforming to the agreement on the cessation of hostilities, the Governments of the two parties will administer respectively the regions which are under their control.

4. Declaration by the delegation of the Democratic Republic of Viet-Nam of the intention of the government of the Democratic Republic of Viet-Nam to examine the question relative to the association of the Democratic Republic of Viet-Nam to the French Union, on the basis of free will, as well as the conditions of such an association. Similar declarations will be made respectively by the Governments of Khmer and of Pathet Lao.

5. Recognition by the Democratic Republic of Viet-Nam as well as by Pathet Lao and Khmer of the fact that France has economic and cultural interests in these States. . . .

6. Pledge by the belligerent parties to refrain from all prosecution of those persons who have collaborated with the opposite party during the war.

7. Exchange of prisoners of war.

8. The implementation of the measures indicated in paragraphs 1 to 7 must be preceded by the cessation of hostilities in Indochina and by the conclusion for that purpose of agreements between France and each of the three countries respectively. Each of the governments must provide:

    a. A complete and simultaneous cease-fire over all the territory of Indochina by all the armed forces—land, sea, and air—of all belligerent parties. In order to consolidate the armistice in each of the three countries of Indochina, the two parties in each case will proceed to a readjustment of the zones which they occupy; in order to assure the aforesaid readjustment, it is equally provided that neither of the two parties will pose an obstacle to passage across its own territory of the troops of the other party in order to rejoin the zone occupied by the latter;

    b. The complete cessation of all introduction into Indochina of new military units, of ground, sea, and air personnel, of all kinds of arms and munitions;

    c. The establishment of a control to assure the execution of the provisions of the agreement on the cessation of hostilities, and the formation to that end of mixed commissions composed of representatives of the belligerent parties in each of the three countries.

After presenting these proposals, Pham added: "It is common knowledge that in order to re-establish peace in Indochina, it is necessary to put an end to the provision by the United States of arms and munitions to Indochina, to recall the American missions, advisors, and military instructors, and to cease all intervention by the United States, in whatever form, in the affairs of Indochina."[25]

The French delayed their response, claiming that the DRVN proposals would inevitably lead to Communist governments in Indochina. Shortly thereafter, in Paris, the opposition pressed for a prompt debate on the Indochina question, and Laniel survived a vote of confidence by a margin of two votes.[26]

Nguyen Quoc Dinh, head of the delegation from the State of Vietnam, presented his government's proposals at the third plenary session, held on May 12:

A. Military Settlement

1. The delegation of the State of Viet-Nam declares itself ready to examine any working document submitted to the Conference for this purpose. These documents must present a serious, positive effort, capable of leading in good faith to a satisfactory military settlement.

2. They must include sufficient guarantees to assure a real and lasting peace, preventing any possibility of new aggression.

3. They must not lead to a direct or indirect partition, final or provisional, in fact or in law, of the national territory.
4. They must provide for an international control of the execution of the conditions of the cessation of hostilities.

B. Political Settlement

With regard to the relations between the State of Viet-Nam and France:

These relations will be settled on the basis of the Joint Franco-Vietnamese Declaration of April 28, 1954. . . .

With regard to the internal political settlement in Viet-Nam:

1. By reason of the territorial and political unity of Viet-Nam, recognition of the principle that the only State legally qualified to represent Viet-Nam is the State embodied by His Majesty Bao Dai, Chief of State. This State alone is invested with the powers deriving from the internal and external sovereignty of Viet-Nam.
2. Recognition of the principle of a single army for the whole territory. This army is the national army placed under the control and the responsibility of the State of Viet-Nam. Settlement of the status of the Viet Minh soldiers within the framework of the legal army of the State of Viet-Nam, in conformity with the principle referred to above and in accordance with methods to be determined. International control of the implementation of the aforesaid settlement.
3. Within the framework and under the jurisdiction of the State of Viet-Nam, free elections throughout the territory as soon as the [U.N.] Security Council verifies that the authority of the State is established over the whole territory and that the conditions of liberty are fulfilled. To assure the freedom and honesty of these elections, international control functioning under the auspices of the United Nations.
4. Representative government formed under the aegis of His Majesty Bao Dai, Chief of State of Viet-Nam, after the elections and in accordance with their results.
5. Pledge by the State of Viet-Nam to refrain from all prosecution of those persons having collaborated with the Viet Minh during the hostilities.
6. International guarantee of the political and territorial integrity of the State of Viet-Nam.

7. Assistance by the friendly nations in order to develop the national wealth and to raise the standard of living in the country.[27]

Bedell Smith immediately endorsed this plan without comment or qualification. Chou En-lai, in contrast, voiced his support for the DRVN proposals. Eden, who chaired the opening sessions, noted that many of the speakers seemed to differ on the history of the conflict, but he observed, "If we differ on history, I hope that does not mean we must disagree on what should be done now." After the session had adjourned, Eden proposed that talks subsequent to the coming fourth plenary session be conducted in closed session.[28]

At the fourth plenary session, on May 14, Soviet Foreign Minister Molotov accused the United States of seeking to expand rather than conclude the Indochinese war and cited increasing U.S. military aid to France. Molotov further claimed that Britain, France, and the United States were attempting to dominate the region militarily in order to crush indigenous national liberation movements and in order to reinforce the Western colonial structures in Asia. After endorsing the DRVN proposals with the suggestion that a neutral international supervisory commission be established to oversee the cease-fire (rather than joint committees of the belligerents), Molotov also endorsed the French suggestion of a conference guarantee of an eventual settlement with collective measures for implementation.[29]

Meanwhile, on May 12, the Laniel government had decided to find out what the United States would do if France could not obtain an honorable settlement at Geneva or if the situation in the Red River Delta deteriorated drastically. The U.S. reply was secret, but the fact of the demarche became known, and press reports speculated about Franco-American military discussions and what the United States might do if things went badly for the West at Geneva.[30]

DISCUSSION QUESTIONS

1. *What were the major points of disagreement between the French, DRVN, and SVN proposals?*
2. *Were there any areas of agreement between the three proposals?*
3. *Should the representatives of the Pathet Lao and the Khmer Issarak have been allowed to participate? How would the increase in the number of actors affect the conduct of the negotiations?*
4. *What options, apart from military intervention, could the United States have pursued if France did not achieve "an honorable settlement"?*

REACHING AN AGREEMENT

Agreements and Disagreements

After the talks moved into restricted session on May 17, several issues emerged as the primary points of discussion. The first concerned the status of the Pathet Lao and the Khmer Issarak and the nature and extent of the hostilities in Laos and Cambodia. Pham Van Dong and Chou En-lai insisted that the Pathet Lao and the Khmer Issarak be recognized, invited to Geneva, and consulted in any negotiations affecting their respective countries. The Western negotiators rejected this argument, and no resolution to this problem emerged from the first several weeks of talks.[31]

On the question of a military versus political settlement to the hostilities in Vietnam, the delegates agreed—after a compromise by Molotov on May 17—upon the former as the initial goal, with the hope that the latter would thereby be made more attainable. They also agreed that a joint military commission composed of representatives of the belligerents should be created to formulate methods for regrouping military forces in Vietnam and for regulating the size and location of regroupment areas.[32]

Around May 23, Eden informed his diplomatic counterparts at Geneva that Britain would withdraw from the conference if results were not forthcoming within two weeks.[33] At the restricted session on May 25, Pham Van Dong, with Soviet and Chinese support, proposed, in regard to regroupment zones, "an exchange of territories, taking account of the following elements—area, population, political interests, and economic interests—in such a way that it gives each party a zone all in one block, relatively extensive, offering facilities for economic activity and administrative control in each zone respectively." The Vietminh, he assured the conference delegates, would not attempt to expand their position militarily once the conference had agreed on a satisfactory end to hostilities. Nguyen Quoc Dinh, head of the SVN delegation, objected to the DRVN proposal, as did Bidault.[34]

By mid-June the conference appeared to have reached a deadlock over two primary points of disagreement. Chou demanded that hostilities in Laos and Cambodia be discussed in tandem with questions regarding the Franco-Vietnamese hostilities. In making this statement he reiterated his demand that the legitimacy of the Pathet Lao and Khmer Issarak be recognized by the conference at large. Furthermore, Molotov reversed his mid-May concession and agreed with Chou that political issues had to be resolved simultaneously with military questions.[35]

External Developments

While the conference delegates discussed the composition and method of a cease-fire oversight body, the Vietminh pressed their military advantage by moving rapidly into the Red River Delta in Tonkin, where French Union forces maintained their defense perimeter. Within this region were the cities of Hanoi and Haiphong. Navarre was forced to order substantial withdrawals to stabilize his position on the delta. By mid-June, the Vietminh had gathered sufficient forces for a heavy strike against French Union defenses, and the French decided to husband their strength by further contracting their defense perimeter.[36]

Meanwhile, on June 4, France and the State of Vietnam had initialed both a treaty of independence of the State of Vietnam, recognizing it as a "fully independent and sovereign State," and a treaty of association between France and the State of Vietnam, calling for the two states to "associate freely within the French Union." The conditions of the association were to be negotiated at a later date. Both treaties were to come into force on the date of signature.[37]

During these weeks the United States made several efforts to clarify its stance. On June 8, Dulles assured the press that "the United States has no intention of dealing with the Indochina situation unilaterally, certainly not unless the whole nature of the aggression should change."[38] Two days later, during an address in Seattle, Dulles charged that Ho Chi Minh was a "Moscow-indoctrinated Communist." Although admitting that the Vietminh had "attracted much genuine native support," Dulles argued that they were so dependent on external Communist support "that if any of the peoples of Vietnam, Laos, or Cambodia should now end in the control of Ho Chi Minh, they would not, in fact, be independent." Dulles then pointed out that there existed several conditions for the creation of a defensive alliance in Southeast Asia: "At the head of the list of those conditions was the stipulation that there must be assurance that the French will, in fact, make good on their July 3, 1953, declaration of intention to grant complete independence [to the Associated States]. The United States will never fight for colonialism."[39]

The following day, June 11, Dulles outlined the conditions which "might justify intervention" in Indochina: "(1) an invitation from the present lawful authorities; (2) clear assurance of complete independence to Laos, Cambodia, and Viet-Nam; (3) evidence of concern by the United Nations; (4) a joining in the collective effort of some of the other nations of the area; and (5) assurance that France will not itself withdraw from the battle until it is won." According to Dulles, "only if these conditions were realized could the President and the Congress be justified in asking the American people to make the sacrifices incident to committing our nation, with others, to using force to help restore peace in the area." Dulles also noted that overt Chinese aggression in Indochina "would be a deliberate threat to the United States itself," and, in such an event, the "United States would of course invoke the processes of the United Nations and consult with its allies. But we could not escape ultimate responsibility for decisions closely touching our own security and self-defense."[40]

As the conference at Geneva continued, the Vietminh consolidated their position on the Red River Delta. On June 12, the Laniel government lost a vote of confidence by a margin of 306 votes to 293. Laniel submitted his resignation on the following day. French President Rene Coty then called upon Pierre Mendes-France, a leading critic of French involvement in Indochina, to form a new government. On June 17, immediately prior to the vote by the still-divided National Assembly on his appointment as premier, Mendes-France announced that he had set himself a deadline—if he had not won an honorable cease-fire in Indochina within one month (by July 20), he would submit his resignation. Mendes-France received a 419-47 vote of confidence from the assembly and, also assuming the portfolio of minister of foreign affairs, took charge of the French delegation at Geneva.[41]

Almost simultaneously in the State of Vietnam, Bao Dai named Ngo Dinh Diem prime minister on June 17. Diem, who at one time had called for the emperor's abdication, was an ardent nationalist, an anti-Communist, a Roman Catholic, and had agitated energetically against the French presence in Indochina.[42] Tran Van Do was appointed foreign minister and replaced Nguyen Quoc Dinh as the chief of the State of Vietnam's delegation at Geneva.

Meanwhile, on June 15, the United States had announced that British Prime Minister Churchill and Foreign Secretary Eden would be coming to Washington for talks with President Eisenhower. At a news conference the same day, Dulles explained that the United States had not given up its view that the situation in Southeast Asia would be improved by creation of a collective defensive system. Dulles added that he believed that the British felt "that the possibilities of Geneva have been exhausted and that the result is sufficiently barren so that alternatives should now be considered."[43]

Geneva: Stalemate Yields to Progress

At Geneva, tentative agreements were reached on several points over the next few days. On June 16, Molotov proposed that the cease-fire supervisory commission be composed either of two Communist states (Poland and Czechoslovakia) and three noncommunist, nonaligned states (Indonesia, India, and Pakistan) or alternatively, the commission could consist of India,

Indonesia, and Poland. In addition, Molotov returned to his earlier position favoring a military solution over a prior political settlement. The same day, Chou told Eden that he thought he could persuade the Vietminh to withdraw from Laos and Cambodia. Chou also offered Chinese recognition of the royal governments of Laos and Cambodia, provided that no U.S. military bases were established in their territories and that the royal governments establish satisfactory relations with the Pathet Lao and Khmer Issarak. On June 19, the delegates agreed to a French proposal for meetings between the French and Vietminh military commands to discuss the cessation of hostilities in Laos and Cambodia. Vietminh officers would represent the Pathet Lao an Khmer Issarak at these talks.[44]

On June 20, Eden and Bedell Smith left Geneva; Molotov left shortly thereafter; and Chou departed five days later. The conference officially continued, but substantive high-level discussions temporarily halted. During the recess of high-level talks, the French and Vietminh military negotiation continued.

Before leaving Geneva, Chou met Mendes-France on June 23. Chou confirmed the priority of the military over the political aspects of the settlement and expressed support for the Vietminh proposal of relatively large regroupment zones. Mendes-France replied that the key question was the location of the demarcation line between the zones and charged that the Vietminh were demanding a line further south than circumstances warranted. (The Vietminh were pressing for a line at thirteen degrees, forty-five minutes, north latitude; the French insisted on the eighteenth parallel.) Chou stated that the military commission would have to reach agreement within three weeks, after which the foreign ministers would return to Geneva. Mendes-France noted that three weeks should be considered the maximum.[45]

The following day Mendes-France met with his top advisors to formulate his negotiating position. He and his advisers settled upon several primary points: a provisional partition of Vietnam at eighteen degrees north latitude would serve as the basis for an agreement; a military solution would take precedence over a political solution, and thus the date of elections (a political question) would remain unspecified; Haiphong would be retained by the French as long as possible to facilitate evacuation by sea; the possibility of retaining French Union forces in Vietnam would remain open; and negotiations with the Vietminh at Geneva would be expedited. These decisions were communicated to Washington and London, along with a request that the final communique of the Anglo-American talks in Washington state, "in some fashion or other, that if it is not possible to reach a reasonable settlement at the Geneva Conference, a serious aggravation of international relations would result."[46]

While the Geneva Conference was in an effective state of suspension, Churchill and Eden arrived in Washington on June 25 to discuss, in Churchill's words, "a few family matters and to make sure there are no misunderstandings."[47] The United States and Britain agreed on a seven-point joint position as to what they would find acceptable in any settlement the French might make at Geneva. They also agreed to avoid making a formal link between the issue of the European Defense Community and the Geneva Conference.[48] On June 29, Churchill and Eisenhower sent the French the seven-point joint position paper. It stated:

The US Government/HMG would be willing to respect an agreement [on Indochina] which:

1. preserves the integrity and independence of Laos and Cambodia and assures the withdrawal of Vietminh forces therefrom;
2. preserves at least the southern half of Vietnam, and if possible an enclave in the [Red River] Delta; in this connection we would be unwilling to see the line of division of responsibility drawn farther south than a line running generally west from Dong Hoi [about 17 degrees, 30 minutes North latitude];
3. does not impose on Laos, Cambodia or retained Vietnam any restrictions materially impairing their capacity to maintain stable non-Communist regimes; and especially restrictions impairing their right to maintain adequate forces for internal security, to import arms, and to employ foreign advisers;
4. does not contain political provisions which would risk loss of the retained area to Communist control;
5. does not exclude the possibility of the ultimate unification of Vietnam by peaceful means;
6. provides for the peaceful and humane transfer, under international supervision, of those people desiring to be moved from one zone to another of Vietnam; and
7. provides effective machinery for international supervision of the agreement.[49]

Chou reiterated China's position on the situation in Southeast Asia during the lull in the discussions. On June 27, while in New Delhi for talks with Indian Prime Minister Jawarharlal Nehru, Chou remarked at a press conference, "Revolution cannot be exported, and at the same time outside interference with the expressed will of the people should not be permitted." The following day Chou and Nehru issued a joint statement declaring that Vietnam, Laos, and Cambodia "should not be used for aggressive purposes."[50] On his way back to China, Chou met with Vietminh leader Ho Chi Minh on July 5.[51]

Mendes-France informed the National Assembly on July 7 that if no satisfactory settlement could be reached at Geneva, he would, before resigning, submit to the assembly a bill providing for the dispatch of conscript troops to fight in Indochina.[52] On July 8, Dulles announced that neither he nor Under Secretary of State Bedell Smith would return to Geneva. Three days later the State Department explained that the United States had "no way of knowing whether a settlement can be reached and, if one is reached, whether or not it will be acceptable. . . . However, this much can be safely said. The United States will not become a party to any agreement which smacks of appeasement. Nor will we acknowledge the legitimacy of Communist control of any segment of South-East Asia any more than we recognized the Communist control of North Korea."[53]

Mendes-France protested that Dulles's concerns were unwarranted and warned that U.S. absence would undercut French bargaining power at a vital stage in the negotiations. Eden joined in these protests, and he and Mendes-France were able to convince Dulles in meetings in Paris in mid-July that the United States should keep representation at Geneva on the ministerial level. Mendes-France threatened that otherwise France would hold the United States responsible for the failure of the Geneva Conference. On July 14, Dulles and Mendes-France signed a secret statement, which repeated the seven points contained in the Anglo-American statement of June 29 and stated, "The United States, while recognizing the right of those primarily interested [France, the State of Vietnam, Laos, and Cambodia] to accept different terms, will itself be prepared to respect terms conforming to the attached [seven points]. The United States will not be asked or expected by France to respect terms which in its opinion differ materially from the attached, and it may publicly dissociate itself from such differing terms."[54] On his return to Washington, Dulles issued a statement that explained:

> The United States has been concerned to find a way whereby it could help France, Viet-Nam, Laos, and Cambodia find acceptable settlements without in any way prejudicing basic principles to which the United States must adhere if it is to be true to itself, and if the captive and endangered peoples of the world are to feel that the United States really believes in liberty. . . . I believe that we have found a formula for constructive allied unity which will have a beneficial effect on the Geneva Conference. And it carries no danger that the United States will abandon its principles.[55]

Dulles also announced that Under Secretary of State Bedell Smith would return to Geneva.

The Situation in Mid-July

The principal negotiators returned to Geneva in mid-July. With Mendes-France's deadline fast approaching, negotiations consisted chiefly of private meetings among small groups of representatives. By July 17, the talks had resolved some disputes but remained deadlocked on others.[56]

- The French continued to insist that the demarcation line between zones be at the eighteenth parallel; the Vietminh, supported by the Chinese and Soviet delegations, demanded the sixteenth parallel. Between the two parallels were the cities of Hue, Da Nang, and Dong Hoi and a major road connecting the coast with Laos.
- The Soviets refused to consent to the maintenance by any belligerent of enclaves within the territory of the other. Mendes-France, by then reconciled to the loss of Haiphong and Hanoi, demanded twelve months for the withdrawal of French Union forces from the Red River Delta; the Vietminh wanted withdrawal within three months; Molotov argued for no more than six.
- The French, Vietminh, Chinese, and Soviets agreed on all-Vietnamese elections. The French and the British did not want the conference to set a date for the elections; the Vietminh wanted elections within six months of a cease-fire; the Soviets, by the end of 1955.
- As for the composition of the proposed international supervisory commission, Eden had proposed Burma, Ceylon, India, Indonesia, Czechoslovakia, and Poland or alternatively, Poland, India, and Indonesia. France, the United States, Vietnam, Laos, and Cambodia preferred some sort of UN supervision. There was also no agreement on the related question of whether the supervisory commission's decisions would be made by majority vote or would have to be unanimous.
- Although Chou and the Vietminh had agreed that all "foreign" troops were to be withdrawn from Laos and Cambodia, the Vietminh demanded privileges for the Pathet Lao and the Khmer Issarak; the Cambodian government insisted on the surrender of all rebels.
- Chou and the Vietminh had also agreed to French retention of two bases in Laos, which were specified in the Franco-Laotian treaty of October 1953. Other than these bases, Molotov and Chou opposed the establishment of foreign military bases in Vietnam, Laos, and Cambodia and wanted assurances that none of the three states would participate in a military alliance. Eden was willing to agree to the neutralization of Vietnam, Laos, and Cambodia, at least, incorporated into a regional security organization.

- Finally, there was the issue of a conference guarantee for any settlement reached. Molotov and Chou insisted upon U.S. "approval," if not a guarantee of the conference's results. The British and the French also wanted the participating powers to underwrite any settlement reached. Bedell Smith, who had returned to Geneva the day before, outlined the U.S. position during a restricted session requested by Molotov on July 18: "If the agreements arrived at here are of a character which my government is able to respect, the United States is prepared to declare unilaterally that, in accordance with its obligations under the United Nations Charter, and particularly Art. II (4), it will refrain from the threat or the use of force to disturb them, and would view any renewal of the aggression in violation of the agreements with grave concern."[57]

Tran Van Do, head of the SVN delegation, informed the same session that the new government of Vietnam had not had an opportunity to express its views; that it did not agree to the conditions advanced for cessation of hostilities, especially those that implied partition; and that it reserved the right to submit a draft declaration outlining its views in the near future.[58]

ENDGAME

On the afternoon of July 18, Chou met with Eden and proposed that the supervisory commission consist of India, Canada, and Poland. All three Western powers accepted the proposal, and in Eden's words, "from that moment the tangled ends of the negotiations began to sort themselves out."[59] The following day, the delegations began to exchange drafts of the four documents expected to result from the discussions—cease-fire agreements for Vietnam, Laos, and Cambodia and a general conference declaration on Indochina.

On July 20, Mendes-France and Chou discussed the issue of the status of Laos and Cambodia. Mendes-France insisted upon complete independence for the two states; Chou wanted limitations upon the right of the royal governments to enter military alliances. Both leaders, however, agreed that Laos and Cambodia would not be permitted to join any military alliance that did not conform to the provisions of the United Nations Charter.[60]

Later that day, the heads of the British, Soviet, French, Chinese, and DRVN delegations met to discuss final difficulties. Molotov, apparently speaking for Chou and Pham Van Dong as well as himself, suggested the seventeenth parallel as the line of demarcation between the two zones. This line would leave Hue, Da Nang, and the road to Laos in the southern zone. Eden and Mendes-France accepted. After each side had expressed its position on the question of elections—Mendes-France argued for leaving the date unspecified; Pham Van Dong favored six months following a settlement at Geneva—Molotov proposed that elections be held within two years following a settlement. Eden and Mendes-France, who had privately agreed that at least eighteen months would be needed to allow Diem time to consolidate his position in the southern zone, quickly agreed.[61]

At the last moment, Sam Sary, representing the Cambodian royal government, notified the conference that Cambodia would sign neither the cease-fire agreement nor any documents produced by the military commission for Cambodia because they compromised the independence of Cambodia by limiting its freedom to enter alliances and to request military assistance from the United States. With time running out, Molotov announced his willingness to allow Cambodia to request foreign military aid should its security be threatened. Mendes-France then suggested that Laos be accorded equal rights and Molotov agreed. At 3:00 a.m. on July 21 the Vietnamese and Laotian cease-fire agreements were signed; that for Cambodia was signed later in the day. Although Mendes-France's July 20 deadline had passed at midnight, all parties nevertheless considered his obligation met and congratulated him on having achieved his goal.[62]

When the conference met for its concluding session, only one hurdle remained: The previously announced intention of the United States to disassociate itself from any official conference documents. The Chinese and Soviet delegations remained adamant that the United States formally adopt the Geneva agreements. Eden, anticipating a last-minute debacle, suggested, and Molotov agreed, that signatures to the documents be eliminated and that the conference participants merely be listed at the heading of the final declaration. This tactic allowed the conference to conclude its work.[63]

DISCUSSION QUESTIONS

1. Why did the United States and Britain threaten to withdraw from the conference? What effect did their threats have? What do these threats tell you about the use of leverage by certain actors in multilateral negotiations?
2. What is your assessment of Pierre Mendes-France's decision to set July 20 as the deadline for reaching an agreement?
3. What impact did the Washington meeting between Churchill and Eisenhower have on the negotiations in Geneva?

NOTES

1. The conference was originally called to discuss a settlement of the conflict in Korea as well as Indochina. Negotiations on the two subjects were

separate, and deadlock set in early in the Korean phase of the conference, which accomplished little.

2. Dwight Eisenhower, *The White House Years: Mandate for Change, 1953-1956* (Garden City, N.Y.: Doubleday, 1963), 342-344.

3. Anthony Eden, *The Memoirs of Anthony Eden: Full Circle* (Boston: Houghton Mifflin, 1960), 97-100, 229-230; U.S. Department of State, *American Foreign Policy, 1950-1955: Basic Documents* (Washington, D.C.: U.S. Govt. Printing Office, 1960), 2372-2373 (hereafter *AFP, 1950-1955*).

4. George McT. Kahin, *Intervention: How America Became Involved in Vietnam* (New York: Alfred A. Knopf, 1986), 38-39.

5. *Ibid.*, 39-40.

6. Allan W. Cameron, ed., *Viet-Nam Crisis: A Documentary History*, Vol. 1: *1940-1956* (Ithaca: Cornell University Press, 1971), 209-214; Kahin, *Intervention*, 44.

7. Kahin, *Intervention*, 41, 44-45, 56; Robert F. Randle, *Geneva 1954: The Settlement of the Indochinese War* (Princeton: Princeton University Press, 1969), 142-143.

8. Robert J. Watson, *The Joint Chiefs of Staff and National Policy, 1953-1954*, vol. 5 of the *History of the Joint Chiefs of Staff* (Washington, D.C.: Joint Chiefs of Staff Historical Division, 1986), 251-252; Kahin, *Intervention*, 42.

9. Randle, *Geneva*, 29; Cameron, *Viet-Nam Crisis*, 228-229.

10. Randle, *Geneva*, 138-141.

11. Kahin, *Intervention*, 22; Allan W. Cameron, "The Soviet Union and the Wars in Indochina," in W. Raymond Duncan, ed., *Soviet Policy in Developing Countries*, 2d ed. (Huntington, N.Y.: Krieger, 1981), 73.

12. Eden, *Full Circle*, 107; Cameron, *Viet-Nam Crisis*, 279-281; James Cable, *The Geneva Conference of 1954 on Indochina* (New York: St. Martin's, 1986), provides an archivally based account of British views and the British role at the conference.

13. Kahin, *Intervention*, 44-45; Eisenhower, *Mandate for Change*, 338-342.

14. Watson, *JCS and National Policy*, 252-253; George C. Herring and Richard H. Immerman, "Eisenhower, Dulles, and Dienbienphu: 'The Day We Didn't Go to War' Revisited," *Journal of American History* 71 (September 1984), 346-348; Eisenhower, *Mandate for Change*, 344-346.

15. Watson, *JCS and National Policy*, 253-254; Herring and Immerman, "Eisenhower, Dulles, and Dienbienphu," 348-354; Cameron, *Viet-Nam Crisis*, 240-241, 244-245, 281.

16. *AFP, 1950-1955*, 2373-2381.

17. Eisenhower, *Mandate for Change*, 346-347; Randle, *Geneva*, 72-73. The dispatch of these notes was publicly announced.

18. Cameron, *Viet-Nam Crisis*, 236.

19. Eisenhower, *Mandate for Change*, 347-349; Randle, *Geneva*, 73-81.

20. Randle, *Geneva*, 81.

21. Cameron, *Viet-Nam Crisis*, 241-243, 245.

22. Herring and Immerman, "Eisenhower, Dulles and Dienbienphu," 358-362; Eisenhower, *Mandate for Change*, 349-356.

23. Cameron, *Viet-Nam Crisis*, 260.

24. Randle, *Geneva*, 206-207.

25. Cameron, *Viet-Nam Crisis*, 261-264.

26. Randle, *Geneva*, 209-210.

27. Cameron, *Viet-Nam Crisis*, 265-266.

28. Randle, *Geneva*, 212-214.

29. *Ibid.*, 215.

30. *Ibid.*, 219-226. The United States continued to make intervention contingent on the conditions that it had already insisted upon and that the French had already rejected; U.S. Department of State, *Foreign Relations of the United States,* 1952-1954, vol. 13: 1522-1525, 1529-1530, 1534-1536 (hereafter *FR*, followed by year and volume number).

31. Randle, *Geneva*, 228-230.

32. *Ibid.*, 228-229.

33. *Ibid.*, 236.

34. Cameron, *Viet-Nam Crisis*, 267; Randle, *Geneva*, 232, 234.

35. Randle, *Geneva*, 270-271.

36. Kahin, *Intervention*, 51-52; Eisenhower, *Mandate for Change*, 364-365.

37. Cameron, *Viet-Nam Crisis*, 268-271. Neither treaty was ever signed, and neither was ever ratified by the French Republic or the State of Vietnam.

38. *FR*, 1952-1954, 16: 1068.

39. Randle, *Geneva*, 257-258.

40. *AFP, 1950-1955*, 2394-2395.

41. Cameron, *Viet-Nam Crisis*, 275-277.

42. Kahin, *Intervention*, 78-80.

43. Randle, *Geneva*, 280-281.

44. *Ibid.*, 281-283.

45. *Ibid.*, 304.

46. *Ibid.*, 306; *FR,* 1952-1954, 13: 1755-1757.

47. *FR*, 1945, 13: 1728-1729.

48. Eisenhower, *Mandate for Change*, 368-369; Randle, *Geneva*, 296. Mendes-France later agreed to postpone the EDC debate in the French National Assembly until at least July 20.

49. *FR*, 1952-1954, 13: 1758.

50. Randle, *Geneva*, 308.

51. According to later reports, Chou put pressure on the Vietminh to settle on terms the French could accept. This pressure apparently included the threat of cutting off military aid. Cameron, "Soviet Union and the Wars in Indochina," 77, 108.

52. Randle, *Geneva*, 314.

53. *Ibid.*, 315.

54. *FR,* 1952-1954, 16: 1363-1364; Eisenhower, *Mandate for Change,* 369-370; Richard H. Immerman, "The United States and the Geneva Conference," *Diplomatic History* 14 (Winter 1990), 63, pointed out that President Eisenhower was also concerned about undermining the French bargaining position and feared the damage to the U.S. international image.

55. *AFP, 1950-1955,* 2396-2397.

56. The following summary is based on Randle, *Geneva,* 333-337.

57. *FR,* 1952-1954, 16: 1434.

58. *Ibid.*, 1432-1433; Randle, *Geneva,* 338.

59. Eden, *Full Circle,* 159.

60. Randle, *Geneva,* 339.

61. *Ibid.*, 339-340.

62. *Ibid.*, 340-341.

63. *Ibid.*, 341-342.

FURTHER READING

Books

Cameron, Allan W., ed. *Viet-Nam Crisis: A Documentary History,* Vol. 1: *1940-1956.* Ithaca: Cornell University Press, 1971.

Eden, Anthony. *The Memoirs of Anthony Eden: Full Circle.* Boston: Houghton Mifflin, 1960.

Eisenhower, Dwight. *The White House Years: Mandate for Change, 1953-1956.* Garden City, N.Y.: Doubleday, 1963.

Kahin, George McT. *Intervention: How America Became Involved in Vietnam.* New York: Alfred A. Knopf, 1986.

Randle, Robert. *Geneva 1954: The Settlement of the Indochinese War.* Princeton: Princeton University Press, 1969.

Articles

Herring, George C., and Richard H. Immerman. "Eisenhower, Dulles, and Dienbienphu: 'The Day We Didn't Go to War' Revisited." *Journal of American History* 71, 2 (September 1984): 343-363.

Immerman, Richard H. "The United States and the Geneva Conference." *Diplomatic History* 14 (Winter 1990): 43-66.

Morgenthau, Hans J. "The 1954 Geneva Conference: An Assessment." Reprinted in Wesley R. Fishel, ed. *Vietnam: Anatomy of a Conflict.* Itasca, Ill.: F. E. Peacock Publishers, 1968.

3

NEGOTIATING NATO'S DEPLOYMENT OF INTERMEDIATE NUCLEAR FORCES

This chapter describes the events that led to the decision of the North Atlantic Treaty Organization (NATO) in December 1979 to pursue a dual-track approach to nuclear force modernization. NATO's decision to deploy 464 cruise missiles and 108 Pershing IIs in Europe while engaging in arms control negotiations with the Soviets was a landmark in the history of NATO's approach to nuclear war. This case is another example of a *small* multilateral negotiation, whose focus was on *security* issues. It illustrates the special problems involved in multilateral negotiations within military alliances, especially when the goals of individual countries conflict with those of the alliance. The impact of domestic politics on major foreign policy decisions and on the process of negotiation is also highlighted in this study. It demonstrates that during multilateral negotiations, the relative importance and influence of particular actors can change.

This chapter is an edited version of the case study by Don R. Drenth, NATO Negotiations on the Intermediate Range Nuclear Forces, 1977-1979, *Pew case study no. 305.*

DECIDING TO NEGOTIATE

Two events served as a significant prelude to the NATO negotiations to deploy ground-launched cruise missiles (GLCM) and Pershing II missiles in Europe. First, the deliberations over the neutron bomb and then President Jimmy Carter's unilateral decision to cancel production heightened European suspicions regarding U.S. leadership of the alliance and seemed to call into question NATO's unity and ability to make hard decisions. Second, U.S.-Soviet negotiations over the Strategic Arms Limitation Talks (SALT) II caused great concern in Europe, where many believed that SALT II would result in a nuclear imbalance in Europe. Part of the basis for this concern was the apparent willingness of the United States to bargain away cruise missile technology, which might be valuable to the Europeans, without excluding Soviet SS-20 ballistic missiles and Backfire bombers, which could target Europe.

The United States had been considering production of an enhanced radiation weapon (ERW)—colloquially known as the neutron bomb—since the early 1970s. The neutron bomb was designed to kill people through the release of neutrons rather than to destroy military installations through heat and blast: In June 1977 Walter Pincus wrote a news article for the *Washington Post* describing the ERW as "the ultimate capitalist weapon, destroying people but leaving buildings intact."[1] This article generated strong controversy in both the United States and Europe. At the October 1977 Nuclear Planning Group (NPG) meeting, the United States asserted that the neutron bomb had been developed to protect Europe and asked for a consensus that it be produced. However, the European allies were unable to reach a consensus at that meeting. The allies faced many domestic difficulties, including rebirth of national peace movements, and the Soviets launched an effective propaganda campaign criticizing the new capitalist weapon.

When no NATO consensus on the neutron bomb emerged by April 1978, the U.S. administration leaked an announcement that Carter had decided not to produce such a bomb. The British, who had been supportive throughout, publicly reaffirmed their support for the bomb. The West German foreign minister, Hans Dietrich Genscher, immediately flew to Washington and, after meeting with President Carter, publicly announced West Germany's support for the production of the neutron bomb. Nevertheless, on April 7, 1978, Carter deferred production of the neutron bomb.

Although NATO accepted the decision, there was dismay in several NATO capitals. In West Germany and the United Kingdom, opposition parties attacked Carter's decision and publicly questioned U.S. leadership. There was concern that mistrust and loss of confidence in U.S. leadership could damage the cohesiveness of the alliance.[2] Effectively, Carter's decision had pulled the rug out from under his European allies. West Germans felt especially vulnerable as they believed that they had a great deal more at stake than the other NATO allies. They were geographically more vulnerable, and they stood to lose more culturally and economically if detente were disrupted.

The other issue that concerned the Europeans during this period was the SALT II negotiations, which began in late 1972 and continued with little success until 1977. President Carter entered the White House committed to arms control; indeed, his administration seemed very eager to reach an agreement. In mid-1977 the U.S. administration attempted to salvage earlier efforts by proposing a three-part formula for SALT II: a treaty, a protocol of limited duration, and a statement of principles for SALT III. The question of cruise missiles was addressed in the protocol, as were other issues that were too important to defer, yet too difficult to solve definitively in the treaty. The Europeans feared that in their eagerness to conclude an agreement, the Americans might neglect Western Europe's security interests.[3]

The "breakthrough" in September 1977 heightened European concerns because SALT II would include cruise missiles but would exclude the Soviet mobile SS-20 ballistic missiles, which the Soviets had begun deploying in early 1977. These new SS-20s caused great consternation among Europeans. German officials were especially worried that these missiles, which targeted Europe, represented a psychological as well as a new military threat to Europeans.

Cruise missile technology was being developed in the United States, and it appeared to the Europeans that the technology might offer a counterthreat to the SS-20s. Yet, it seemed to the Europeans that the United States was willing to trade cruise missile technology for a negotiated SALT. Further, the air-launched cruise missile (ALCM), which the United States was deploying on its own bombers, was to be treated differently from cruise missiles possibly based in Europe. Finally, the breakthrough would allow provisions for the Soviet Backfire bomber that would ensure its use exclusively against Europe.[4] All these measures could lead the Soviet Union to believe that the security of the United States and that of Europe could be treated separately, and this further heightened European concerns.

NATO's nuclear strategy since its inception had depended upon the U.S. nuclear umbrella. However, the willingness of the United States to use its nuclear weapons and to risk the possible destruction of its cities in defense of Europe had been a continuing source of conflict within NATO. Once the Soviets reached nuclear parity with the United States, European doubts over the U.S. commitment increased and "decoupling" of the United States and Europe became a real concern for many Europeans, particularly the Germans. SALT II, as it was being negotiated, seemed to increase the possibility of decoupling.

During 1977-1978 the United States tried to reassure its allies through closer consultations on SALT II talks and by sharing information on cruise missile technology. The United States argued that the ban on cruise missile deployment had little real effect because testing could still continue, and the protocol would not represent a precedent, nor would it be automatically extended. But the Europeans argued that if cruise missiles were of such little significance, why were they included at all? In order to diminish European interest in cruise missile technology, the United States prepared a paper that outlined the advantages as well as the disadvantages of the cruise missile. The Europeans perceived this as another U.S. effort to sell SALT II; some Europeans wondered why cruise missiles were good for the United States but not for Europe.

In May 1977, NATO decided to review nuclear forces in Europe as part of the alliance's long-term defense planning. During the summer, the United States asked its allies if existing sea-based systems were an adequate link between Europe and the U.S. central strategic deterrent. Both the United Kingdom (UK) and West Germany felt the sea-based systems were no longer adequate. The UK argued that the existing theater capability was based upon an aging land-based (aircraft) force, and additional rungs on the nuclear escalation ladder were necessary to ensure that the doctrine of flexible response remained viable. West Germany believed that the Soviet SS-20 posed a psychological threat to Europe that could not be countered without a NATO modernization program that visibly demonstrated the U.S. nuclear commitment.[5]

The United States remained committed to SALT II but wished to assuage European concerns as well as to demonstrate a strong commitment to NATO. Partly because of European concerns, the Carter administration had decided to proceed with the development of a ground-launched cruise missile. The administration also saw merit to the development of cruise missiles because they could be used as bargaining chips during SALT II negotiations. Others felt that the technology offered military options that had to be protected because it might enhance U.S. strategic retaliatory forces.[6]

REACHING AN AGREEMENT

Negotiations to modernize NATO's intermediate-range nuclear forces began in late 1977 and culminated in NATO's formal decision, which was announced in December 1979. Although bilateral talks obviously played an important role in negotiations, two new ad hoc committees were established by the Nuclear Planning Group (NPG) to deal with two aspects of NATO's nuclear force modernization. The High-Level Group (HLG) was established in October 1977 and was specifically required to examine the role of theater nuclear forces (TNF) in NATO strategy; the ramifications of recent Soviet deployments; the need to modernize; and the military, political, and technical implications of various TNF postures. However, almost from the beginning and largely at European prompting, the HLG focused on the necessity for TNF modernization.[7]

The NPG established the Special Group on Arms Control and Related Matters (commonly called Special Group—SG) in April 1979 as a result of allied concerns about arms negotiations. The committee was designed to provide the Europeans with a greater opportunity for consultations on arms negotiations and was told to work out the negotiating framework for future arms control talks between the United States and the USSR.

Both committees were chaired by the United States and were open-ended which meant that those nations that wished to participate could do so, but a quorum was not required for meetings to take place. All NATO countries except France, Iceland, Luxembourg, and Portugal participated, and membership in both committees consisted of high-level staff members of national governments rather than the national permanent representatives to NATO (who had to work within detailed and restrictive nationally established guidelines). The advantage of this ad hoc arrangement was that representatives to the two committees were the individuals who would be responsible for making the decisions work within their own governments. Further, negotiations were not so rigid as talks normally are within standing committees as delegates were part of their national decisionmaking bureaucracies. Whereas the HLG members came primarily from national defense departments, SG participants normally were from foreign ministries. However, some of the smaller countries used the same representative for both committees, and national representatives to one committee occasionally participated in the other.[8]

The High-Level Group

When the NATO Nuclear Planning Group met in October 1977, both the nuclear force modernization and the neutron bomb were on the agenda. At the NATO summit in May 1977, President Carter had suggested that a major effort be undertaken to improve NATO forces, both conventional and nuclear. The Long-Term Defense Program was primarily designed to improve conventional forces, and only one of the ten task forces was charged with nuclear force improvements. Because of rising European concerns, the United States wished to demonstrate that it took the issue of theater nuclear force modernization very seriously, and at the NPG in October 1977 the United States recommended that the nuclear task force of the Long-Term Defense Program be elevated to a higher level of NATO experts than were participating in the other nine task forces of the review.[9] The NPG accepted the U.S. suggestion and established the High-Level Group. Initially, the United States, the United Kingdom, and Germany were the most active members of the HLG and the key actors in the intermediate-range nuclear forces (INF) negotiations. During the next few months, the majority of the staff work was done by the United States; although the UK occasionally provided input, the other countries participated very little, if at all.[10]

Meanwhile, West German Chancellor Helmut Schmidt, speaking to the International Institute of Strategic Studies in London in October 1977, publicly expressed his concerns about SALT II. He argued that the "strategic parity codified by SALT neutralized the strategic nuclear capabilities of the United States and the USSR and magnified the disparities between the East and West in tactical nuclear and conventional weapons." He commented that if the disparities remained, then the alliance "must maintain the full balance of deterrence strategy . . . and must therefore be ready to make available the means to support its current strategy."[11] The U.S. administration recognized Schmidt's speech as a public expression of European concerns and resolved to use the HLG to work with the Europeans to eliminate their concerns.

The first HLG meeting was held in December 1977. This meeting consisted of briefings and discussions on doctrine and NATO's nuclear capabilities as well as those of the Warsaw Pact. The SS-20 was one of several Soviet systems discussed. The Americans used this first meeting to probe European positions and concluded that consensus on the best course of action would be possible.

When the HLG met again in February 1978, the United States indicated four possible courses of action. First, NATO could resolve to do nothing; this option was quickly dismissed because Europeans wished to ensure that SALT II did not restrict European options on cruise missile technology and because there was a perceived political need to respond to SS-20 deployments. Second, NATO could build a serious battlefield nuclear capability for the theater that would not have the capability to strike targets within the Soviet Union. The Europeans were reluctant to build such a capability, and they agreed that any new capability should strike the Soviet Union. Third, NATO could develop a theater force capable of waging counterforce and counter-value strategic nuclear war against the Soviet Union. European delegates promptly rejected this option because it could be perceived as decoupling U.S. strategic forces from the defense of Europe. Finally, NATO could make modest improvements in the long-range theater nuclear forces. This was attractive because (1) it was a visible response to SS-20 deployments; (2) it did not imply any decoupling; and (3) it was the least provocative and would, therefore, be most acceptable to domestic elites that favored continuation of detente.

However, the HLG still felt new weapons should be able to strike targets within the Soviet Union; therefore, its recommended course of action was a combination of the latter two options. In its initial report to the NPG in April, the HLG recommended an "evolutionary upward" adjustment of NATO's theater nuclear forces that would enhance long-range theater capability.[12]

President Carter's decision to cancel production of the neutron bomb was publicly announced in April 1978, and although the decision did not appear to be directly harmful to the HLG's work, it did deepen mistrust of the United States in NATO capitals, particularly in West Germany. Schmidt had been concerned over erratic U.S. leadership for quite some time and worried that the U.S. commitment to the European allies was weakening. Within the HLG, West German officials supported the need for nuclear force modernization but announced that they were not willing to have new weapons deployed to West Germany under dual control arrangements. (The majority of nuclear weapons deployed to West Germany up to this date were under "dual control," which meant that West Germany controlled the launch vehicles, and the United States retained sole control of the nuclear warheads.) This position may have been due partially to Schmidt's distrust of Carter, but the position also made it easier for Schmidt to support detente.[13]

The neutron bomb episode also increased U.S. doubts about the Europeans' ability to make politically tough decisions and stick to them. U.S. recommendations on nuclear issues had previously been accepted with relatively little debate. Carter and other administration officials had seen the neutron bomb as a test of the Europeans' abilities to take a more active role in nuclear policy matters in the alliance. Some concluded that domestic problems caused them to fail the test; such a failure should not be repeated. Now that allies were seeking to have a more active role in nuclear force modernization, some U.S. officials worried that the allies' domestic problems would again impede decisionmaking, effectively demonstrating the increasing lack of NATO unity.

Although the U.S. Defense Department had accepted the need to modernize since the February 1978 HLG meeting, others were unconvinced until after the cancellation of the neutron bomb.[14] On both sides of the Atlantic there was agreement that NATO appeared to lack the cohesiveness necessary to carry out politically tough decisions, and some U.S. officials, particularly in the State Department, became convinced that modernization was necessary to erase any such appearance to the Soviets. Furthermore, they argued, it was important to demonstrate strong leadership to the Europeans, who were uncertain of U.S. resolve. Support for modernization in the United States grew as a result of political requirements; it was also a perceived military need.

In January 1979, the heads of state of France, West Germany, the United Kingdom, and the United States held a summit on Guadeloupe. They reviewed the neutron bomb episode and agreed that such an event should not be allowed to recur. There was concern that the Soviets' propaganda campaign against the neutron bomb had worked, and there was general agreement that there needed to be a show of alliance unity. The possible need for NATO to modernize theater nuclear forces might be the opportunity to demonstrate the alliance's cohesiveness. To demonstrate his support for NATO and his willingness to consider his allies' viewpoints, Carter offered cruise missile technology and the modernized Pershing II as systems for NATO modernization. At the conclusion of the summit, the four leaders agreed that the best approach would be for NATO to pursue a dual-track approach to future nuclear deployments: modernization and future arms control.

In the meantime, the HLG had been reviewing the options for force modernization. The U.S. chairman focused the HLG's work on possible adjustments to the theater nuclear forces that could be supported by available and developing technology.[15] The UK wished to consider the new cruise missile technology for two reasons: First, it appeared useful for NATO modernization; and, second, the UK had begun a review of its own nuclear deterrent and there was interest in cruise missiles as a possible replacement for the UK's aging Polaris. Other allies expressed interest in the cruise missile technology because it would meet the criteria established as well as meet the SS-20 threat.

U.S. officials had been reluctant to concentrate solely on cruise missile technology because the United States had not defined a role for cruise missiles in its own arsenal. However, after the January summit, the HLG began focusing on cruise missiles and Pershing IIs.

After the January summit, Carter sent David Aaron, the deputy national security adviser, to Europe to brief the allies on the U.S. position, based upon the HLG's work. The purpose of Aaron's trip was to build a strong European consensus for modernization in order to neutralize domestic pressures to the greatest extent possible. However, although the British remained strong supporters, there was already some ambivalence forming in West Germany. The faction within the Social Democratic Party (SPD) that had opposed the neutron bomb because of its potential damage to detente was likely to oppose modernization on the same grounds. Schmidt believed that he could control this faction, but he needed assurances that the United States would pursue arms control of the long-range theater nuclear forces. Further, he reiterated the condition that Germany not be the only continental nonnuclear ally to accept new weapons on its soil.[16]

Aaron made another trip to Europe in March 1979 and found that concern over potential modernization had grown. In the Netherlands and Belgium, officials acknowledged the political need for a visible NATO response to Soviet SS-20 deployments; yet, because of domestic political problems, they were reluctant to endorse modernization publicly. Instead, they preferred to wait until a formal NATO decision was imminent before they chose to tackle the issue. Schmidt had recently overcome SPD opposition to modernization during a parliamentary debate. To acknowledge SPD concerns over potential damage to detente, he pressed strongly for arms control initiatives.

In contrast, British and Italian support for modernization was high. Despite internal problems, Prime Minister Francesco Cassiga argued that Italian support for modernization would bolster Italy's role in NATO and assure Italy of inclusion at future summits. Further, the Italian Socialist Party made the potential nuclear deployments a test of the Italian Communist Party's stated loyalty to NATO.[17]

By early spring 1979, the HLG concluded that the modernization of the nuclear force should be a mixture of ground-launched cruise missiles and Pershing IIs, but the actual numbers to be deployed had not yet been decided. Although sea-based cruise missiles had been considered, they were rejected for several reasons. Land-based missiles would represent a more visible "coupling" of the United States and Europe and would leave the Soviets with no doubt that a nuclear strike on Europe would result in a retaliatory nuclear attack on the USSR. Land-based systems would afford deliberate escalation and selective use, whereas sea-based missiles would not. There were command and control problems with a sea-based system, and there were doubts over whether viable participation by the allies could be worked out. Also, costs would be considerably higher if new ships had to be built to carry the sea-based missiles. Pershing II was viewed as a replacement for Pershing I, already deployed in Germany, and Pershing II was not designed to be deployed at sea. Therefore, if cruise missiles were sea-based, Germany would be the only country with modernized land-based missiles on its soil that could reach deep into Soviet territory. This was unacceptable to Germany. There was also concern that ships that carried the sea-based systems would be the target for political protest when they put into port. The United States felt that sea-based systems avoided risk sharing whereas land-based systems were visible indications of risk sharing. Also, sea-based systems were viewed as an impediment to arms negotiations because they would complicate the talks.[18]

In early summer 1979, the HLG settled on a deployment of 572 nuclear weapons (464 ground-launched cruise missiles (GLCMs) and 108 Pershing IIs). The Pershing IIs (PIIs) would replace the 108 Pershing Is already based in West Germany, which were under U.S. control, whereas the GLCM force represented a new force.

The exact number of 572 represented a compromise of political and military arguments that suggested forces varying in size between 200 and 600. The number had to be large enough to constitute a political response by

NATO as well as to ensure military credibility. That meant that it had to be large enough to withstand a possible Soviet preemptive strike and to penetrate Soviet air defense. Yet it could not be so large as to provide a separate theater nuclear capability because that could be perceived as decoupling the United States from Europe. Further, the number had to be large enough to encourage the Soviets to negotiate arms reduction seriously and to provide a margin for reduction of the new forces through negotiations, but it could not be so large that it was perceived by the allies' publics as an escalation of the arms race.

The HLG also wished to maximize difficulties for Soviet planners while enhancing NATO flexibility, and it had to consider Germany's refusal to be the only country to accept new weapons. Pershing was fast and accurate, but its range made it unfeasible for deployment to other countries. The GLCM was slower but had a longer range, and therefore it would be suited to deployment to the UK and Italy, where governments were favorably disposed to accepting missiles on their soil.

The HLG felt that the mixture of 464 GLCMs and 108 PIIs offered a force of high accuracy and one with complementary characteristics that enhanced NATO options: (1) it provided flexibility to select the best weapon for a given mission while complicating Soviet planning; and (2) the mixed force provided a hedge against failure of one type of system. Also, the mix spread the nuclear risk among the allies and gave NATO the capability to attack a wider range of targets from several different NATO bases.[19]

Once the HLG had decided on the hardware, it concentrated on basing locations. After a process of elimination based largely on national political concerns, five countries were left for consideration: West Germany, the United Kingdom, the Netherlands, Belgium, and Italy. Once these nations became candidates for basing, their role in HLG negotiations increased. This was particularly the case for Belgium and the Netherlands. For one thing, their willingness to support a final decision and base missiles on their soil became a significant factor in NATO's success. Without their support, there could be no consensus and NATO might appear unable once again to make and carry out a politically difficult decision. Also, the countries themselves had an even greater interest because of the potential impact on their national governments.

The Dutch government faced the most difficult domestic situation. Dutch parliamentary debates on nuclear issues had been intense. The government, a coalition of the Christian Democratic Appeal (CDA) and the Party for Freedom, had a very slim majority of two votes in the Second Chamber. A majority of the CDA and the Party for Freedom as a whole favored deployment. The main opposition party, Labor, was strongly opposed. In fact, the Labor Party congress held in late April 1979 suggested that the Netherlands should consider leaving NATO if the neutron bomb were subsequently approved for deployment in Europe. They also called upon NATO to adopt a no-first-use policy and stated that there should be no conventional buildup to replace withdrawn nuclear missiles.[20] National elections were not due to take place until May 1981, but enough CDA members were opposed to deployment that a vote to deploy new weapons would be defeated and could bring down the government.

The Belgian coalition government had been preoccupied with internal conflict between the Flemish and Walloon communities, as well as serious economic problems. Although there was deep division over socioeconomic issues within the government, only the Communist Party was publicly opposed to a nuclear arms buildup. As the year went on, however, the coalition government became more concerned with arms control and potential basing in Belgium. Belgian representatives had participated in HLG discussions and were essentially supportive of modernization, but they argued for tangible arms control efforts.

Despite Italian enthusiasm, the United States remained doubtful about Cassiga's ability to maintain a favorable climate for basing. Italy had had a great number of coalition governments, and the current one seemed no more secure than previous ones. However, the INF question was not a divisive domestic issue. Indeed, Italy remained eager to prove its loyalty to NATO by agreeing to base the new missiles on its soil.

West Germany also had a coalition government, consisting of a Social Democratic Party (SPD) majority and a Free Democratic Party (FDP) junior partner. However, a sizable number of SPD members felt that arms control was more important than modernization. The FDP, in contrast, was convinced that modernization was necessary to offset a growing imbalance and an increasing Soviet threat. The chancellor, Helmut Schmidt, recognized that in order to gain his party's full support, every effort must be made to protect West German relations with the Eastern bloc, and to that end, arms control efforts must equal modernization efforts. That year was an especially difficult one for Helmut Schmidt. He was committed to detente and arms control, but he also saw the need for new weapons to counter the SS-20 threat. Although he was still distrustful of U.S. leadership, he agreed that NATO needed to demonstrate its ability to make hard political decisions and stick with them.

Antinuclear movements were also growing in 1979, especially in the Netherlands, the United Kingdom, and Germany. The most substantial antinuclear movement was in the Netherlands, where it had strong backing from the church and was very broadly based. The UK Campaign for Nuclear Disarmament (CND) had been essentially dormant since the late 1960s, but was now receiving some political support from the left wing of the Labor Party.[21] However, CND was not viewed as a formidable force in 1979, especially since the Conservative Margaret Thatcher government had won a substantial majority in the May 1979 election.

In Germany, however, the peace movement had strong historical and cultural roots. In the late 1970s it became linked with the strong environmental protection movement (the Greens). It was extremely active and received support from a variety of groups, i.e., those that favored detente, those that really were pacifist, and those that dreamed of reunification. The rise of peace protests gave the German Communist Party an opportunity to emerge from isolation, and its members added support to the peace movement.[22]

As the HLG continued its work in 1979, several countries expressed concern that a formula of hardware without arms control would be difficult to sell to their peoples. Germany especially wished to see deployment tied to arms control. The Dutch argued for arms control first and deployment only if arms talks failed. Denmark and Norway, in keeping with strong pacifist traditions, also advocated arms control negotiations. The NPG took note of these countries' concerns and established the Special Group on Arms Control in April 1979.

The Special Group

The Special Group (SG) was given the job of working out the negotiating framework for future arms control talks between the United States and the USSR. This gave the Europeans, particularly those countries that believed arms control efforts should precede any decision on deployment of new weapons, an avenue for greater input into the arms control negotiations. Because the domestic political climates were changing, the SG could also be viewed as an effort to calm public anxiety and make an eventual deployment decision more palatable.

It is ironic that the European allies who had expressed concern with SALT II in 1977 came to view it by mid-1979 as the basis for future arms control. United Kingdom and German officials believed that ratification of SALT II would ease the way for the deployments, whereas the Dutch felt that U.S. Senate ratification of the treaty was essential for their participation. By September 1979, the SG concluded that arms talks on reduction of long-range theater nuclear forces should take place within the SALT framework and should give primary attention to the Soviet land-based missile force, as it was the most immediate threat to Europe.

DISCUSSION QUESTIONS

1. Which countries were the key actors at this stage of the negotiations? Why are these countries influential at this stage of multilateral negotiations?

2. *Was it necessary to establish the High-Level Group (HLG) and the Special Group (SG) on Arms Control and Related Matters? What do the HLG and SG tell you about the use of groups and committees in multilateral negotiations?*
3. *Why did the HLG decide that deploying 572 land-based missiles was the appropriate option?*
4. *What other military options to land-based missiles were available?*

NEGOTIATIONS INTENSIFY

The HLG and the Special Group met in Brussels in late September to complete their final reports. The NATO general secretary, Joseph Luns, called a special joint meeting of the two groups on September 28 to ensure that the two separate reports were mutually consistent and complementary. They were subsequently combined into the Integrated Decision Document (IDD). The draft IDD and the two separate reports were forwarded to the nations concerned; these documents were discussed at the November meeting of the permanent representatives to NATO and formed the basis for the formal ministerial decision in December 1979.

Meanwhile, the USSR was conducting a propaganda campaign to prevent any modernization of existing NATO forces. The campaign alternated veiled threats with efforts to cajole the Western public into refusing new weapons on their soil. The Soviets insisted that parity existed and adopted a divide-and-conquer approach. Although they concentrated their efforts on influencing West German opinion, none of the allies was neglected.[23]

During his visit to Berlin on October 6, 1979, Leonid Brezhnev offered to reduce Soviet medium-range systems in Eastern Europe if NATO did not implement its modernization decision. He announced Soviet resolve never to use nuclear arms against those states that renounced the production and acquisition of such arms and did not deploy the new weapons on their territory. At the same time, Brezhnev declared that West Germany must decide for itself whether it wished to aggravate the European situation by deploying new U.S. missiles on West German soil. He stressed that such a decision would worsen West Germany's position and it would not be difficult to predict the consequences for West Germany if the weapons were used. Brezhnev then offered to withdraw 20,000 troops and 1,000 tanks from East Germany.[24]

Both West Germany and the Netherlands argued that Brezhnev's offer should receive serious consideration. Italy and the United States initially rejected the offer, but then Carter appeared to change his mind and declared his willingness to explore Brezhnev's offer. Carter's announcement was hailed by West Germans as a sign that the United States was open to arms reductions without installing additional weapons as bargaining chips.

However, Brezhnev's offer received a cool response from the UK.[25] The defense minister, Francis Pym, remained concerned about the state of NATO's theater nuclear forces. He was also concerned about the state of British forces after the reductions under the earlier Labor government. Indeed, the UK government increased its efforts to state publicly the need to modernize NATO's long-range theater nuclear force, as well as to enhance Britain's own independent deterrent. There was little government opposition, and even though CND was growing, public opposition was still fairly low.

The situation was quite different on the Continent, however. On October 11, 1979, the Dutch Second Chamber debated the proposed modernization. Even though there was no general resolution, news reporters suggested that a large majority of the Second Chamber was opposed to making a decision until the U.S. Senate ratified SALT II. Political parties were split on the best way to proceed. The Party for Freedom and some members of the Christian Democratic Appeal argued for support for the NATO decision, but Labor believed that the decision could be delayed for almost a year. Some of the left-wing members of the Christian Democratic Appeal maintained that 1983 would be early enough for NATO to make a final decision. To add more fuel to the controversy, Max Van der Stoel, a former Labor Party foreign minister, had returned from Moscow on October 9, 1979, to report that the Soviet Union had rejected a moratorium on production of the SS-20s during potential SALT negotiations regardless of what NATO's decision would be.

A few days later, the *New York Times* reported that the West Germans were pressuring the Dutch to support modernization. Apparently, the Germans believed that Dutch support would deflect Soviet charges that West Germany had pressed on with deployment despite strong Dutch opposition. Dutch support would also assuage left-wing German Social Democrat reservations over deployments. Klaas De Vries, the chairman of the Dutch parliament's Defense Commission, reported that the West Germans felt that Belgian and Italian participation was not sufficient, and he predicted that the United States would have to prod the West Germans into accepting new weapons. De Vries also stated that the current nuclear deterrent was credible and did not require modernizing.[26] Bonn quickly denied that Dutch participation was essential to West German participation and notified the Carter administration of West Germany's continuing support.

To demonstrate U.S. commitment to arms control, the Carter administration had been working on a draft arms reduction proposal to limit long-range systems in Europe. In mid-October 1979, David Aaron flew to Europe to consult the NATO allies on this draft. Within the administration, there were hopes that the draft would assuage European fears and ease the way for modernization. In fact, Aaron was also told to press the allies for full support of INF deployments to the five countries. Privately, however, several members of the Carter administration believed that they would not get European support for deployment without an arms control offer.[27]

On November 1, the Dutch press reported that the Labor Party and the Party for Freedom were strenuously opposed to the CDA's stance in favor of separating the manufacture and the deployment of new nuclear weapons in NATO's decisionmaking. After a lengthy debate on October 31, the Dutch parliament had not reached a decision, but according to news reports, it was clearly moving toward holding negotiations before a decision to modernize was made.

On November 2, newspapers reported that the Labor Party Second Chamber group had voted almost unanimously in favor of postponing the decision on modernizing nuclear weapons—a vote that would make the cabinet's decision even more difficult. The Christian Democratic Appeal was considering a conditional agreement on separate decisions on stationing and deploying the missiles, but the Party for Freedom, the coalition partner, wanted unconditional support for modernization so that negotiations would proceed from that position.

On November 7, the Labor Party, the country's biggest single political party, publicly called on the Dutch parliament to oppose NATO's efforts to modernize nuclear forces as well as the stationing of nuclear weapons in Holland. It further proposed that NATO withdraw 2,000 warheads in return for drastic reductions in Soviet SS-20s. Bram Stemerdink, a former defense minister, argued that an arms balance existed and that it was therefore unnecessary for NATO to make a decision to modernize at the meeting scheduled for December 12.

On November 8, Dutch papers reported that the cabinet had agreed that modernization was a prerequisite for arms negotiations with the Soviets. Dutch Foreign Minister Christoph Van der Klaauw argued that failure to reach a decision on modernization would damage the U.S. negotiating position in talks with the Soviet Union and said that the objective in the negotiations should be the "mutual zero option": The negotiations should ultimately aim to achieve the mutual dismantling of medium-range nuclear weapons in Europe. Van der Klaauw reiterated the importance of SALT II and repeated that the government could not make any unconditional promise on modernization without ratification of SALT II. He went on to announce that, at Holland's initiative, NATO was studying an exchange of short-range nuclear weapons for medium-range nuclear weapons. Moreover, NATO had promised not to increase the overall number of nuclear weapons in Europe anyway. Finally, he announced that the United States had recently proposed a reduction of nuclear weapons in Europe by an additional 1,000 warheads. Yet Van der Klaauw refused to promise the Dutch people that his government would back a modernization decision only after parliamentary consent.[28]

In Brussels, *Le Soir* carried a statement by the Flemish People's Union chairman that denounced the deployment of cruise missiles on Belgian soil. He argued that the deployment was "strategic and aggressive," and he advocated a gradual reduction in the armaments of the two big military blocs. He went on to say that Belgium's decision on basing was vital because it would determine the position that West Germany and the Netherlands would take.[29]

The UK maintained its public support for a NATO decision to modernize. Defense Minister Pym held a news conference with U.S. reporters and told them that the Western media had paid too much attention to Brezhnev's offer. He expressed strong support for SALT II, but he stated that his priority was reaching agreement with the other European partners on the deployment of cruise missiles.[30] For the first time, Pym revealed that the missiles would probably be located at two or three bases in the UK beginning in 1983.

The national defense ministers gathered in the Hague on November 13-14, 1979, to discuss the proposed modernization. The Dutch suggested informally that NATO approve production of the weapons but delay the deployment decision for two years in order to determine the success of negotiations. The Americans argued that deployment and production could not be separated; Congress would be most unwilling to approve production unless the allies had formally agreed to accept the missiles. The Dutch proposal gained no real support among the other allies. Although Belgium and Denmark also favored a delay, the consensus of the group was that the USSR would not negotiate seriously unless the new weapons were actually in the pipeline.[31]

The United States, the UK, and West Germany viewed a total consensus as essential to demonstrate NATO unity, and there was hope among the group that the Dutch could be persuaded to go along with NATO's decision by reducing the overall Dutch nuclear role in NATO. Yet the allies recognized that if the Dutch took a positive stand on production and deployment, the coalition in power could fall apart; a new Labor-led coalition would be adamantly opposed to modernization. Several delegates were predicting that the Dutch would agree to the deployment in principle but would refuse to base them on Dutch soil.[32] The U.S. and West Germany were concerned that if that happened, Belgium might also decline to accept the weapons and the entire plan could fall apart before it got started.

Three thousand demonstrators gathered at the Hague on November 17 to stage a protest against NATO plans to install cruise missiles in the Netherlands. The Dutch cabinet publicly delayed any formal decision until December 7. On November 28, the permanent representatives to NATO met to review the draft IDD as a valid basis for the ministerial decision to be taken at the December meeting of the NATO ministers. The Dutch again expressed their reservations and suggested a delay in the decision. The draft was approved, however, and placed on the ministers' agenda for the December 11-12 meeting.

On December 5, Dutch Prime Minister Andries Van Agt announced that he would meet with Belgian Prime Minister Wilfred Martens to try to gain Belgian support for postponement of the NATO decision. He also planned to meet with UK Prime Minister Margaret Thatcher and Italian Prime Minister Cassiga to solicit their support.

On December 7, the Dutch Parliament rejected production and deployment by a vote of 76-69. Van Agt was out of the country; he and the Norwegian prime minister had flown to Washington to emphasize the importance of real negotiations with the Soviets and reiterate their concerns with modernization. Carter advised both that he felt modernization was necessary but that he was willing to reduce the number of weapons deployed if the USSR would reduce its arsenal. He urged them to support the deployment, emphasizing the importance of maintaining cohesion within the alliance. Denmark's foreign minister was also in Washington for talks with Secretary of State Cyrus Vance, and he proposed a six-month delay in the deployment decision so that NATO could seriously consider the Soviets' arms proposal. Vance reiterated the same points that Carter had made to the two prime ministers.

The Belgian parliament publicly voiced doubts about the intended deployments, and the Socialist Party, during its annual meeting, voted for delay. U.S. officials acknowledged worry about a domino effect as the Dutch fears spread to other countries, leaving NATO in disarray. Nevertheless, there was some hope. Despite strengthening domestic opposition, the Italian parliament approved the deployment plan. The UK remained its strongest advocate. In West Germany, on December 6, the Social Democratic Party reelected Helmut Schmidt chairman by a vote of 365-38 (17 abstentions). The party congress had been a vitriolic affair, and Schmidt had threatened to resign if the SPD did not support NATO's position; Schmidt's reelection was interpreted by U.S. officials as a clear German mandate to go ahead with the deployment.

In an effort to unify NATO for the upcoming decision, Carter publicly announced on December 8 that he was prepared to cut back on the deployment numbers if the USSR would agree to reduce its own arsenal. At the same time, U.S. officials disclosed that the Soviets had deployed 120 SS-20 missiles in East Germany and that intelligence reports indicated that more than 100 additional missiles were likely to be produced in the very near future. Without the NATO deployments, U.S. officials charged, there would be a great imbalance in Europe.

Van Agt went to Bonn to state his case. But he got no support; Schmidt agreed with the United States that without a positive decision on deployment, NATO would be forced to negotiate from a position of weakness. Van Agt returned home facing the potential downfall of his government. Although parliament had voted against deployment, the Party for Freedom threatened to bring down the government if the cabinet voted with the parliament.

The NATO meeting was scheduled for December 11-12; and the press reported that Pym was coming to the meeting determined to get NATO to move swiftly. He reiterated that the deployments were essential in response to the Soviet buildup. Van Agt was in a very tenuous position, with little apparent appreciation for his position on the part of his allies. Yet, Dutch opinions carried considerable weight, and the United States still hoped to find a way to get Dutch agreement for the decision.

DISCUSSION QUESTIONS

1. *Should NATO have accepted Brezhnev's offer?*
2. *What was the impact of domestic considerations on the positions of allied governments during this period of the negotiations?*
3. *What impact would a ratification of Salt II have had on the allies?*

ENDGAME

At the start of the two-day meeting, the United States maintained its position that a firm declaration without reservations was essential to demonstrating alliance unity. Although well aware of the Netherlands' domestic problems, U.S. officials believed that if the Dutch were allowed a formal reservation, then the Belgian government would press for the same. Because the Belgian and Dutch governments remained shaky, a political crisis in Italy, where the government was also somewhat shaky, could leave the West Germans on their own in deploying new weapons—an outcome they had consistently pledged to reject. On the margins of the meeting, there were bilateral talks with the various countries lobbying for their particular point of view.

In the United States, SALT II was still in trouble, and Carter attempted to ease its difficulties by agreeing to give the Senate a more direct role in SALT negotiations. Some senators had given conditional support for SALT II, support based on increased defense spending. Senator Sam Nunn had demanded a preview of Carter's proposed defense budget before the vote on SALT. Carter was still personally committed to SALT, and he was well aware that the vote on SALT II would have a critical impact upon the NATO decision. In a White House speech on December 12, 1979, he outlined his fiscal 1981 defense budget proposal for $142 billion, which represented a growth of about 3.5 percent after inflation.

During one of the formal NATO ministerial sessions, the Dutch read a carefully prepared statement. In essence, the statement said that the Dutch recognized the need to respond to Soviet deployments, especially of the SS-20 and the Backfire; however, in view of the importance of arms control and the unilateral goal of zero option, the Netherlands could not commit itself to deploying cruise missiles on its territory. The Dutch deferred their final basing decision until December 1981 and said that it would be taken in light of specific results in the arms limitation talks. The spokesperson went on to say that any deployment of new systems on Dutch soil must lead to a reduction in existing nuclear roles. Furthermore, this decision assumed that SALT II would be ratified; without SALT II the matter would have to be reconsidered. Finally, he emphasized that the final Dutch decision would require the support of the Dutch parliament.[33]

The Belgian government went along with the NATO decision in principle but opted to review its decision to base missiles on Belgian soil six months later. The decision would be reviewed in the light of progress in arms limitation.[34]

On December 12, after seven hours of debate behind closed doors, NATO announced its dual-track decision. The official communique noted the Warsaw Pact's increased nuclear capability, particularly the Soviet deployment of SS-20s and the Backfire bomber, whereas the Western long-range theater nuclear force remained static. In order for NATO's strategy of flexible response to remain credible, NATO needed to take concrete steps, and the ministers had concluded that the overall interests of the alliance were best served by two parallel and complementary approaches to TNF modernization and arms control.

Regarding deployment, 572 weapons (464 cruise missiles and 108 Pershing IIs) would be deployed. One thousand weapons currently in Europe would be withdrawn as soon as possible, and the new weapons would be deployed within that lower ceiling, in a one-for-one swap. The communique said that NATO believed that arms control was essential to a more stable East-West military relationship as well as to advancing detente.

The communique also noted the intensive consultations among the NATO allies with respect to arms control and gave full support for the U.S. decision to negotiate arms limitations on long-range theater nuclear forces with the Soviets as soon as possible. The NATO ministers did, however, place several limits on those talks. First, limitations on U.S.-European theater weapons must be balanced by limitations on Soviet theater systems. Second, U.S.-Soviet negotiations should take place in the context of SALT II in a step-by-step approach. Third, the immediate objective of negotiations should be agreed limits on land-based long-range theater nuclear forces. Finally, any agreement must provide equality in ceilings and sites and must be adequately verifiable. In light of any concrete results reached through negotiations, NATO's theater nuclear force requirements would be reexamined. The Special Group was replaced by a Special Consultative Group to ensure continued allied communication with U.S. negotiators dealing with the Soviets.[35] Of the fourteen nations represented, only two (Belgium and the Netherlands) had expressed formal reservations about the dual-track decision.

The next day, Prime Minister Van Agt read the Dutch formal statement at the NATO meeting to his own parliament. After reading this statement verbatim, Van Agt clarified several points. First, production of new weapons had not been a point of contention. Second, modernization was not new but was the outcome of a lengthy study. Third, at Dutch and West German initiative, NATO had set up another committee to deal solely with arms limitation. Fourth, the Dutch position outlined in his formal statement was taken only after it had been ascertained that the other NATO allies could not endorse other ideas offered by the Netherlands. Finally, he assured parliament that this position had not damaged the Netherlands' standing within NATO. Although it was a carefully developed position designed to save the government, Van Agt's critics predicted that the government would soon fall.[36]

In the British Parliament, Defense Minister Pym hailed the decision as a demonstration of the cohesion and political will of NATO in response to the Soviet threat. Several members of Parliament called for a full debate; the opposition leader asked for assurances that the United States would not make any decision on the missiles without consultation with the UK government, and Pym gave this assurance. Otherwise, reaction was muted.

For the first time in the history of NATO, the Europeans had jointly decided on an issue concerning nuclear warfare: Weapons that could reach deep into the Soviet homeland would be positioned in Europe. Despite previous misgivings about U.S. leadership and in view of their own domestic concerns, the NATO allies had reached a decision in which they were deeply involved. They would remain deeply involved as the decision was carried out. NATO would face a multitude of problems regarding the dual-track decision, but for the moment, NATO had shown its resolve and its unity.

DISCUSSION QUESTIONS

1. *Why was reaching a decision by consensus important to U.S. policymakers?*
2. *Could Belgium and the Netherlands have been dissuaded from lodging formal reservations to the decision? What do these reservations reveal about the difficulty of multilateral negotiations within alliances?*
3. *What alternatives to a dual-track decision did NATO have?*

NOTES

1. Walter Pincus, *Washington Post* (June 7, 1977).
2. S. T. Cohen, *The Neutron Bomb: Political, Technological and Military Issues* (Cambridge, Mass.: Institute for Foreign Policy Analysis, Inc., November 1978), 53.
3. Marsha McGraw-Olive and Jeffrey D. Porro, eds., *Nuclear Weapons in Europe: Modernization and Limitation* (Lexington, Mass.: Lexington Books, 1983), xvi.
4. Gregory F. Treverton, "NATO Alliance Politics," in Richard K. Betts, ed., *Cruise Missiles: Technology, Strategy, Politics* (Washington, D.C.: Brookings Institution, 1981), 419-422.
5. *Ibid.*, 424.
6. Robert J. Art and Stephen E. Ockenden, "The Domestic Politics of Cruise Missile Development," in Betts, *Cruise Missiles: Technology, Strategy, Politics*, 393-405.
7. J. Michael Legge, *Theater Nuclear Weapons and the NATO Strategy of Flexible Response* (Santa Monica, Calif.: Rand Corporation, April 1983), 35.
8. Paul Buteux, *Strategy, Doctrine and the Politics of Alliance* (Boulder: Westview Press, 1983), 123-125. Chapter 4 provides an authoritative, comprehensive analysis of the roles of the NPG, HLG, and SG in NATO nuclear negotiations regarding INF.
9. Legge, *Theater Nuclear Weapons*, 34.
10. Treverton, "NATO Alliance Politics," 427.
11. Helmut Schmidt, The 1977 Alastair Buchan Memorial Lecture before the International Institute for Strategic Studies, October 1977. Reprinted in *Survival* (International Institute for Strategic Studies, January-February 1978).
12. David N. Schwartz, *NATO's Nuclear Dilemmas* (Washington, D.C.: Brookings Institution, 1983), 217-219.
13. *Ibid.*, 219.
14. *Ibid.*, 224.
15. Stephen R. Hanmer, Jr., "NATO's Long Range Theater Nuclear Forces: Modernization in Parallel with Arms Control," *NATO Review* (February 1980), 4.
16. Schwartz, *NATO's Nuclear Dilemmas*, 228-229.
17. *Ibid.*, 229-230.
18. John Cartwright and Julian Critchley, *Cruise, Pershing and SS-20* (London: Brassey's Defence Publishers, 1985), 16-18.
19. *Ibid.*, 10-16.
20. Charles Batchelor, "Anti-nuclear Move in Holland," *Financial Times* (May 1, 1979), 2.

21. Gregory Flynn and Hans Rattingen, *The Public and Atlantic Defense* (Totowa, N.J.: Rowman and Allanheld, 1985), 12.

22. Diana Johnstone, *The Politics of Euromissiles* (London: Verso, 1984), 53.

23. Cartwright and Critchley, *Cruise, Pershing and SS-20*, 15.

24. Guido Vigveno, *The Bomb and European Security* (Bloomington: Indiana University Press, 1983), 102-103.

25. "Caution Over Soviet Offer," *Financial Times* (October 10, 1979), 12.

26. John Vinocur, "Bonn Links Basing of Missile to Dutch," *New York Times* (October 18, 1979), 1.

27. Richard Burt, "Missile Bid to Dutch Is Denied by Bonn," *New York Times* (October 19, 1979), 9.

28. "Cabinet Firm on NATO Modernization," *Handelsblad* (November 8, 1979), 1 (FBIS translation).

29. "VU Chairman Opposes NATO Missile Deployment Plans," *Le Soir* (November 10, 1979), 2 (FBIS translation).

30. R. W. Apple, "Britain Is Studying New Nuclear Force," *New York Times* (November 11, 1979), 17.

31. Michael Getler, "10 Allies Favor New Missiles but Dutch Still Waver," *Washington Post* (November 14, 1979), 21.

32. Michael K. Burns, "NATO Unity Indicated on Nuclear Additions," *Baltimore Sun* (November 14, 1979), 4.

33. "Verbatim Text of Van Agt Statement," *Handelsblad* (December 13, 1979), 3 (FBIS translation).

34. Walter Taylor, "NATO Members Approve Sites for New US Missiles," *Washington Star* (December 13, 1979), 1.

35. "Communique Issued at a Special Meeting of the NATO Foreign and Defense Ministers in Brussels on 12 December 1979," in Cartwright and Critchley, *Cruise, Pershing and SS-20*, Annex A, 151-153.

36. "Dutch Cabinet Periled on Missiles," *New York Times* (December 20, 1979), 2.

FURTHER READING

Books

Betts, Richard K., ed. *Cruise Missiles: Technology, Strategy, Politics.* Washington, D.C.: Brookings Institution, 1981.

Buteux, Paul. *Strategy, Doctrine and the Politics of Alliance.* Boulder: Westview Press, 1983.

Cartwright, John, and Julian Critchley. *Cruise, Pershing and SS-20.* London: Brassey's Defence Publishers, 1985.

Coker, Christopher. *The Future of the Atlantic Alliance*. London: Macmillan Press, 1984.

McGraw-Olive, Marsha, and Jeffrey D. Porro, eds. *Nuclear Weapons in Europe: Modernization and Limitation*. Lexington, Mass.: Lexington Books, 1983.

Schwartz, David N. *NATO's Nuclear Dilemmas*. Washington, D.C.: Brookings Institution, 1983.

Articles

Garthoff, Raymond L. "The NATO Decision on Theater Nuclear Forces." *Political Science Quarterly* 98, 2 (Summer 1983): 197-214.

Hanmer, Stephen B. "NATO's Long-Range Theater Nuclear Forces: Modernization in Parallel with Arms Control." *NATO Review* (February 1980): 1-6.

Kelleher, Catherine McArdle. "The Present as Prologue: Europe and Theater Nuclear Force Modernization." *International Security* 5, 4 (Spring 1981): 150-168.

Treverton, Gregory F. "Nuclear Weapons and the 'Gray Area.'" *Foreign Affairs* 57, 5 (Summer 1979): 1075-1089.

4

NEGOTIATIONS AT UNCTAD I

The United Nations Conference on Trade and Development held in 1964 was the first international conference devoted to North-South issues. In contrast to the first two case studies in this volume, it is an example of a multilateral negotiation that focused on economic, trade, and development issues, and with over 100 states represented it is an example of a *large* multilateral negotiation. It demonstrates the contending views of global economic relations of the less developed countries (LDCs) and those of the industrialized world. An important factor in the negotiations was the *asymmetry* in the wealth and power of the participants; it therefore offers insights into multilateral negotiations among unequal actors in the international system. The differences among the various members of the Group of 77 (G-77) and the Western Group, particularly the United States, draw attention to the challenges to unity that confront *negotiating blocs*. This case is also useful for discussing the ways in which UNCTAD I laid the foundations for future UNCTAD conferences and affected the evolution of the North-South dialogue.

This chapter is an edited version of the case study by Carol Lancaster, The United States at UNCTAD I, *Pew case study no. 108.*

DECIDING TO NEGOTIATE

The first United Nations Conference on Trade and Development (UNCTAD) began in March 1964 and concluded in June of the same year. The conference, attended by over 2,000 delegates from 120 countries, was called to discuss trade problems relevant to economic development of less developed countries (LDCs).   On the conference agenda were proposals involving trade preferences for manufactured goods exports from developing countries to developed-country markets, commodity price stabilization, increased resource transfers to LDCs, reductions in freight and insurance charges for LDC trade and in LDC debt repayments, and the creation of new international machinery to provide a forum for continuing discussion of trade and development issues. Of all these issues, that of trade preferences was the newest and the most prominent. During the conference, proposals in all these areas were discussed and resolutions negotiated. These resolutions were then voted on by participating countries.

UNCTAD I was the first real international conference of all members of the UN dedicated exclusively to considering North-South issues. A number of officials from LDCs indicated that for them, this conference was the "most important international event . . . since the founding of the United Nations."[1]

In the aftermath of UNCTAD, assessments of the U.S. role in the conference were uniformly negative. One academic from Canada wrote: "The United States appeared to lack both an understanding of the basic needs of the less developed countries and any desire to gain one. An American observer remarked of the chief delegate of his country: 'He had nothing to offer and so he offered nothing.'"[2]

A prominent U.S. economist commented on the impression the United States had left in the wake of UNCTAD I: "Increasingly the United States has appeared to be isolated from the general trend of thinking and discussion about problems of the less developed countries, a long vice of negation confronting a chorus of hopeful positive suggestions. This was certainly the impression registered on the other participants and the observers and commentators at UNCTAD."[3] These and other comments reflect what was at best a diplomatic embarrassment for the United States and at worst, a diplomatic defeat at UNCTAD I. What had happened and why?

The World in the Early 1960s

The call for an international conference on trade and development was first made in the early 1960s. These were years when global political issues revolved around two principle axes: relations between rich, northern industrialized countries and the poorer, southern developing countries; and relations between the Western democracies and the countries of the Socialist bloc. The evolution of the North-South dialogue will be described later. In East-West relations at this time, Cold War competition was particularly intense. The Soviets had demonstrated their ability to compete with and, indeed, lead the West in space by orbiting the first space capsule in the late 1950s. They had begun to compete for influence in the Third World with their support of Fidel Castro's revolution in Cuba and their warming relations with several newly independent African countries. The conflict in Indochina between Socialist North Vietnam and Western-backed South Vietnam was intensifying and increasingly absorbed U.S. personnel, resources, and attention as the 1960s progressed.

UNCTAD I grew out of a proposal for convening a world conference specifically to discuss the economic problems of less developed countries, first made in the declaration of nonaligned countries at Belgrade, Yugoslavia, in September 1961. The proposal resulted from the growing sense of dissatisfaction among LDCs with existing international institutions—above all the General Agreement on Tariffs and Trade (GATT)—in addressing their development needs. The GATT had been set up in the early postwar period, when the attempt to create an International Trade Organization failed for lack of U.S. support. The GATT was really an agreement among members—mostly developed countries of Europe, North America, and Asia, though a number of developing countries were also members—governing their trade practices. Two fundamental principles included in the GATT were nondiscrimination in trade and the promotion of free trade through negotiating the removal of trade barriers, such as quotas and tariffs. Negotiations among members were normally based on reciprocity—an exchange of reductions in trade barriers. In the early postwar years, LDCs had taken relatively little interest in the GATT. Barriers to agricultural exports, which many of them produced, were exempted from GATT negotiations, largely because the United States and several other developed countries had elaborate domestic farm income-support programs, coupled with protection of their agriculture against imports. Additionally, many LDCs felt they could not afford to trade reductions in their own tariffs or quotas for similar reductions from other countries, as their tariffs were often an important source of government revenue. Moreover, both tariffs and quotas were employed to protect newly established industries in developing countries, which, it was believed, could not survive and become efficient without protection from foreign imports. (This is the famous "infant industry" argument.)

In the early 1960s, most less developed countries were poor, with per capita incomes below $300 per year. Their economies were based on the production and export of primary products, such as coffee, cocoa, copper, or cotton. Many of them, especially the poorer ones in Africa, still relied to a degree on foreign aid to finance a proportion of their annual investment. However, they were not all alike. A number of the more advanced LDCs, such as Brazil, Korea, and other Asian and Latin American countries, had growing industrial sectors and were beginning to export manufactured goods.

The call for an international conference on trade and development was also a part of what had already become, in effect, a North-South dialogue between developing and developed countries; in this dialogue the former made proposals to the latter on a range of issues designed to promote the economic development of LDCs and exerted whatever pressures they could in multilateral fora to obtain developed-country support for their proposals. Such proposals were statements of broad principles but usually implied action by developed countries to provide benefits (largely in the field of trade and aid) to LDCs, which would not be obligated to provide reciprocal benefits to developed countries.

The North-South dialogue on development issues began in the United Nations after World War II. As early as 1946, developing countries that were members of the UN (primarily from Latin America) argued for increased aid in the form of technical assistance. In 1948, the LDCs employed for the first time a tactic that they were later to use frequently. In one of the committees of the General Assembly, they simply voted—over the opposition of developed countries—to allocate funds from the annual budget of the UN for the provision of technical assistance to LDCs. (This possibly historic vote was 26 in favor, 11 opposed, and 12 abstaining.) Later, after corridor discussions, a resolution was passed in the plenary session of the General Assembly to "appropriate the funds necessary for the Secretary General to provide technical assistance." As this resolution had no specific money figures associated with it, developed countries agreed not to oppose it, and it passed 46-0-6.

During the 1950s, discussions and negotiations in the UN on North-South issues continued. One of the major issues during this period involved increased aid to developing countries through a World Bank reorganized so that the developing countries would have predominant voting power. When it became clear that developed countries would not agree to such a reorganization, LDCs began to focus on setting up an alternative institution, called a Special United Nations Fund for Economic Development (SUNFED), which would be financed through contributions from developed countries and in which all member states would have one vote. After several years of discussions and studies, the LDCs made it clear in a meeting of the UN Economic and Social Council in 1957 that later that year at the General Assembly meeting, they would go ahead and vote to set up the SUNFED, whether developed countries were willing to support it or not. In fact, the Soviets had promised to support it and were rumored ready to contribute $25 million. France, Denmark, Holland, and several other developed countries also expressed their support. Faced with the prospect of being outvoted, possibly isolated, and left out of an organization that might conceivably get off the ground, the United States proposed an alternative–the creation of a new UN program of expanded technical assistance in LDCs. This proposal was passed by the General Assembly that year, and the SUNFED proposal was temporarily put aside. U.S. Under Secretary of State C. Douglas Dillon explained the U.S. proposal as an element in a broader UN negotiating strategy:

> Last year the situation was such in the United Nations that if we had not been able to find an alternative and one which we thought was a good alternative, and one we could sell to the other countries, the United Nations would have undoubtedly voted the creation of SUNFED to which we were very much opposed, for it would put the United Nations in the development business. We certainly could not have gone along with that and would not have contributed to it, for we felt that would have caused us a very severe propaganda defeat in the underdeveloped areas because the Soviets were ready to go along.[4]

However, U.S. officials recognized that their tactic of proposing an alternative to SUNFED would not permanently eliminate the issue from the political agenda of the LDCs. As one of them put it, "I do not mean to suggest that this [i.e., the U.S. proposal] will forever stay this persistent demand for some further capital for development purposes, but I think it has met the situation at least for the time being."[5]

Less developed countries did revive their pressures in the UN and elsewhere for establishing a UN capital development fund. But the intensity of these pressures began to diminish after the creation of the International Development Association, the soft-loan window of the World Bank, in 1959 and with the growing interest among developing countries in trade as a vehicle for their development.

Trade issues had been in the forefront of economic issues of concern to developing countries since the Havana Conference in 1947-1948 which attempted to create an International Trade Organization (ITO). (That organization was never established, largely because of the unwillingness of the United States to ratify the treaty negotiated in Havana. U.S. unwillingness was in significant part a result of the sections of the treaty charging the ITO with responsibility for promoting commodity price stabilization through international commodity agreements.)

Primary Product Producers

Developing countries were exporters mainly of primary products, the prices of which tended to surge or drop with the weather or with speculative demand. Not surprisingly, developing countries were eager to promote international action to stabilize the prices of their primary product exports. However, by the 1950s, concerns with commodity prices began to take on an added dimension. After the commodity boom of the early 1950s stimulated by the Korean War, primary product prices had begun to decline relative to the prices of manufactured goods. Raul Prebisch, executive secretary of the Economic Commission for Latin America, produced a theory to explain this trend and had a major influence on the thinking of intellectuals and government officials in developing countries. He argued that because of differences in elasticities in demand and supply for primary products and manufactured goods and the different characteristics of the markets for these goods (the former being highly competitive and the latter oligopolistic or monopolistic), productivity increases in primary products were passed on to consumers in the form of lower prices, whereas productivity increases in manufactured goods production were retained by the producers in the form of higher profits. Thus, argued Prebisch, there was a secular trend for the terms of primary producers to deteriorate.

There were several policy implications of Prebisch's analysis. First, developing countries would have to reduce their reliance on primary product exports and industrialize if they were to realize the benefits of growth. During this period, many governments in developing countries adopted policies of import-substituting industrialization as a first step in their development, providing high protection for enterprises in their countries that produced manufactured goods to substitute for imports. LDCs also pressed hard in international fora, particularly in the UN, for the establishment of international commodity agreements that would stabilize and raise the prices of their exports. In most cases, the emphasis was on raising commodity prices above international market equilibrium levels, in effect forcing an income transfer from consumers of such commodities (mostly developed countries) to the producers (the LDCs).

The United States was the most outspoken opponent of international commodity agreements, regarding them as unworkable and likely to result in rigidities and distortions in international trade. U.S. opposition continued until the early 1960s, when the new Kennedy administration, acceding to pressures from Latin American countries, agreed to join the International Coffee Agreement and President John F. Kennedy himself declared at a meeting in Costa Rica that the United States was "willing to move ahead on agreements stabilizing the prices of other commodities."[6] Economic and political development in the Western Hemisphere was an important objective in the early years of the Kennedy administration, reflecting in part concerns over the presence of Fidel Castro in Cuba and the potential expansion of Cold War competition to Latin America implied by Castro's close relationship with the Soviet Union. Despite President Kennedy's speech, the United States remained unenthusiastic about commodity agreements and particularly opposed to such agreements if their objective was to raise prices above world market equilibrium levels.

By this time, however, another trade issue had gained prominence on the LDC agenda—the expansion of LDC exports to developed countries. It was becoming clear that foreign aid was not going to increase dramatically regardless of pressures by developing countries. And in many countries, opportunities for import-substituting industrialization had already been exploited, not always with hoped-for results. Instead of reducing imports, new enterprises had often increased imports by creating a demand for spare parts, raw materials, and capital goods (all of which had to be purchased from abroad) to maintain and increase their production. Moreover, high levels of protection of these "infant industries" had often continued (even after they were well established), resulting in inefficient and high-cost production and in products that were more expensive and of lower quality than similar goods produced abroad. Finally, a number of developing-country economies were small and likely to remain so, given their small populations and land area. These countries were thus prevented from exploiting the scale economies in a number of industries that would help make them efficient. They clearly needed larger markets through exporting abroad. One approach that became popular among developing-country officials, particularly in Latin America, was to expand LDC markets through economic integration schemes, for example, the Central American Common Market or the Latin American Free Trade Area. The success of these schemes was never certain, however. Hence, the LDCs put considerable emphasis on the obvious alternative, i.e., to expand exports to developed-country markets.

Throughout the 1950s, LDCs had pressed for improved access to developed-country markets for their exports generally. Developed countries usually responded by advising them to pursue such issues in periodic trade negotiations organized by the General Agreement on Tariffs and Trade. LDCs found GATT to be dominated by developed countries and issues of importance to them. For example, appeals by LDCs for lower tariffs on their agricultural exports fell on deaf ears as developed countries erected tariff barriers and established quotas to protect their farmers and effectively agreed among themselves not to negotiate on agricultural trade in GATT-organized trade rounds. Similarly, although developed-country members of GATT frequently affirmed the importance of nondiscriminatory free trade, when developing countries threatened to compete seriously with domestic U.S.

producers (as in the case of textiles), developed countries raised a variety of protectionist barriers against developing-country imports. As a result, the LDCs increasingly regarded the GATT as a "rich man's club," where their interests and influence were marginal. By the end of the 1950s, support was increasing among LDCs for creating a new international trade organization focused specifically on their concerns.

By the late 1950s, the issue of improved access to developed-country markets had become one of preferential access to those markets for LDC exports. When the European Economic Community (EEC) was formed in 1957, it was agreed that the colonies of member states, the Associated Overseas Territories (AOTs), would be given special access to the EEC market for their products. This arrangement paralleled the existing preferential access to the market of the United Kingdom for its former and current colonies. The provision of preferences to the large and promising EEC market for a number of African producers alarmed governments in Latin American countries whose exports, particularly of tropical beverages, competed with those of African colonies. The Latin Americans as well as officials from developing countries elsewhere in the world feared being excluded from the EEC market and began to lobby for expanded preference arrangements to include them.

By the early the 1960s, the increasing prominence of trade and development issues, added to the growing dissatisfaction among LDCs (whose numbers were rapidly increasing with the independence of African countries) with the abilities of existing international institutions to deal with their needs, resulted in an LDC-supported proposal in the UN to convene the first Conference on Trade and Development.

DISCUSSION QUESTIONS

1. *Why did North-South issues come to a head in 1964?*
2. *Should issues of trade and development have been dealt with multilaterally?*
3. *How did developing countries perceive the international economic system?*
4. *What were the major differences between the United States and the LDCs?*

REACHING AN AGREEMENT?

When resolutions were introduced in the UN General Assembly in 1961 to convene a trade and development conference, the United States opposed them. The idea of a conference was strongly supported by the Soviets, who had long been critics of the GATT (they were not members) and who had advocated the creation of a new world trade organization to include them.

Only after a direct appeal by the U.S. ambassador to the United Nations, Adlai Stevenson, to President Kennedy to reverse the U.S. position did the United States agree to a resolution requesting the secretary-general to consult governments for their views on the need for such a conference. Once it became clear that such a conference would take place, the United States continued to regard it as "no more than a diplomatic hurdle to be overcome somehow, with no expectation of positive gain when the other side had been reached."[7]

UNCTAD I was held between March and June 1964. The principal issues raised at UNCTAD were outlined in a report by Raul Prebisch, entitled *Towards a New Trade Policy for Development*, prepared as part of the documentation for the conference. In this document, Prebisch reiterated his arguments about the tendency for the terms of trade of primary producers to deteriorate over time and the consequent importance of diversification into industrial production. His policy recommendations included the establishment of price-stabilizing commodity agreements, compensatory finance schemes for developing countries suffering drops in their export earnings, reduction or elimination of developed-country barriers to trade in agricultural goods, the creation of regional economic groupings among developing countries to promote industrialization and trade, and the granting by developed countries of preferential access to their markets for industrial exports from developing countries.

The conference was organized into five committees to deal with the following issues: international commodity problems; trade in manufactures and semimanufactures; the cost of invisibles (insurance, freight, debt servicing) to LDCs; institutional arrangements; and regional economic groupings among LDCs.

The committee on commodities was to consider measures for stabilizing commodity prices at "fair and remunerative levels"–i.e., establishing and maintaining a parity between prices of primary products and prices of manufactured goods. This approach was intended to stabilize the terms of trade of primary products rather than simply the prices of their exports. Most economists and U.S. officials found this idea an anathema, a threat to free markets and efficient resource allocation. Even the LDCs recognized its limitations, especially in encouraging the development and use of synthetics if primary product prices were increased to sufficiently high levels. Consequently, LDCs supplemented this proposal with one calling for compensatory financing to be established initially to provide resource flows (preferably automatic and preferably in grant form) to offset sudden decreases in the LDC's foreign exchange earnings. The idea of establishing a compensatory finance scheme was introduced into UN discussions when a 1954 report by experts proposed that a compensatory finance facility be set up under the auspices of the International Monetary Fund (IMF). The IMF representative at the UN discussion took the position that existing fund programs were adequate to meet LDC needs for compensatory finance and that no new scheme was needed. In the UN in 1958, Brazil introduced the idea again of establishing a compensatory finance scheme (a link with the fund was not mentioned), and it was agreed that a committee of experts would study the idea. In their 1961 report, the experts proposed the creation of a new Development Insurance Fund to provide compensatory finance, funded by developed countries. In 1963, the IMF established its own program of compensatory finance, in part as an effort to preempt the establishment of such a fund independent from the IMF. Thus, by the time of UNCTAD I, the issue had lost much of its urgency.

The committee on trade in manufactures and semimanufactures was to focus on the issue of preferences—the newest and most controversial issue at UNCTAD I. Prebisch argued that preferential access to developed-country markets for semimanufactures and manufactures from LDCs was an extension of the "infant industry" argument, whereby newly established industries, which initially were small and had inexperienced managements, needed special advantages (i.e., preferences as well as protection) to be able to compete. Once they were established and had expanded their production to take advantage of scale economies, they would become cost efficient and no longer need special arrangements. If developed countries wanted to promote LDC trade and development, preferential access to their markets was an important means of doing so.

Despite the intuitive appeal to developing countries of preferential access for their industrial products to the markets of developed countries, there was considerable controversy on whether preferences would in fact provide significant benefits to LDCs and what form of preferences would be both equitable and practical. On the impact on LDCs of preferences, one analyst pointed out that the advantages of preferences would likely be small, given the degree of preferential access being proposed (e.g., 50 percent lower tariffs for imports from LDCs in developed-country markets than for similar imports from developed countries). Preferences would have an even more modest impact after the substantial reductions in tariffs expected from the Kennedy Round of tariff negotiations, then under way. This analyst further argued that those manufactured goods that could most benefit from preferences, e.g., textiles and footwear, were precisely the ones that were least likely to be awarded preferences because of the threats they presented to domestic producers in developed countries.[8] Another economist argued that preferences might well benefit developing countries, but only if they were regarded as a form of aid rather than commercial policy, and that, in any case, the value of preferences for developing countries required further study before it could be assessed conclusively.[9]

On the form that preferences might take, two basic types of preferential arrangements were proposed. The first type, favored by many developing countries, was a system of generalized preferences, applied by all developed countries to all semimanufactures and manufactures of all developing countries. The objective of this type of preference scheme would be to avoid discrimination among LDC producers or developed-country importers. However, there were a number of difficult problems associated with the creation of such a scheme. First, some LDC exporters clearly did not need preferences to compete in developed-country markets, as demonstrated by the success of Korea, Taiwan, and others in penetrating the U.S. and European textile markets. For the less competitive countries to benefit equitably from preferences, they would have to have proportionately greater preferences or else the preferences for more competitive LDCs would have to be limited. Another problem related to the developed countries providing the preferences. All such countries would have to provide a similar degree of preference to LDC imports to ensure that the burden of adjusting to the inflow of industrial products from LDCs was not unfairly borne by those countries granting more generous preferences. But how should a "similar degree of preference" be calculated, given the different levels of protection in individual developed countries? Finally, should existing preferences enjoyed by developing countries be eliminated without compensation?

Another type of preferences proposed by the Belgian minister for external trade, Maurice Brasseur, was a "selective system," which would involve the negotiation of preferences between individual LDCs and developing countries according to the needs and opportunities of both. This approach would avoid all of the contentious issues associated with a generalized system of preferences, but it too had disadvantages. It would be extremely cumbersome to implement, given the large number of potentially eligible products, the large number of LDCs that would be interested, and the number of developed countries with which they would have to negotiate their preferences. Such a scheme provided no guarantee of equitable treatment of LDCs or equitable burden-sharing among developed countries. Indeed, such a scheme would lend itself to political manipulation by developed countries and could result in increased dependence on developed countries by benefiting LDCs.

The committee focusing on invisibles and insurance was to consider ways to reduce charges to LDCs for shipping, insurance, and debt servicing. Proposals considered in this committee were neither new nor so contentious as those discussed in other committees.

A fourth committee was to deal with institutional arrangements, specifically, the establishment of "continuing machinery" to focus on trade and development issues in the future. A fifth committee was to examine issues associated with regional economic arrangements among LDCs to promote intra-LDC trade.

DISCUSSION QUESTIONS

1. *Why was the United Nations chosen as the forum for this conference?*
2. *Was President Kennedy correct in reversing earlier U.S. opposition to the conference?*
3. *Why were committees used at this stage of the multilateral process? Was the use of committees effective?*
4. *If only a few LDCs would benefit from preferences, why was preferential access strongly supported by the Group of 77?*

ENDGAME

In the months preceding UNCTAD I, the LDCs made considerable efforts to prepare themselves on the issues and to coordinate their negotiating positions and strategies. Prebisch and other experts produced documents and briefed key developing-country delegations on major issues. The developing countries themselves met regionally to produce common positions. The problems of shaping a common position among at least 77 independent countries (known as the Group of 77 [G-77]), with a diversity of economic needs, goals, and conditions, can be easily imagined. In order to develop such a position, every country had to have something to gain. Thus, for the poorer countries, the issues of more foreign aid and commodity stabilization were important. Negotiations among the G-77 were arduous, and language on especially contentious issues was left vague. The negotiations also involved extensive logrolling (the trading of votes by legislators to secure favorable action on projects of interest to each one) and, as a result, were very rigid. To alter agreed-upon positions would require further extensive negotiations among the G-77 to ensure that everyone still had something to gain and that the coalition remained intact.

At the preparatory committee for UNCTAD, the developing countries presented a joint resolution elaborating a unified position on trade and devel-opment issues for the upcoming conference, including the progressive elimin-ation of all barriers impeding the exports of manufactured goods from LDCs; increased aid; reduction in LDC payments for freight, insurance, and debt servicing; and the establishment of "new machinery and methods for imple-menting the decisions of the conference."

However, the apparent unity among the G-77, particularly on the issue of preference, was fragile. These countries that already enjoyed preferential access to developed-country markets—principally the Commonwealth countries and the newly-independent African countries that had in 1963 signed the Yaounde Convention continuing their preferential access to the EEC market—were reluctant to give up their preferences. This had been demonstrated by their vote against the principle of generalized preferences in GATT in 1963.[10] Their later votes with the G-77 in support of a generalized system of preferences were in favor of very broad statements of principle with contentious issues of detail avoided. The Latin Americans, in contrast, were strongly against preferences for special groups of LDCs and had made repeated pleas to the EEC (with U.S. support) to have preferences extended to them. When their requests had come to naught, they appealed to the United States to provide them special compensatory preferences in the lucrative U.S. market. In fact, what individual LDCs were likely to want depended in considerable part on what developed countries decided to do. In the words of one observer, "India favors general preferences and the United States favors nondiscrimination. Were the United States to shift its position to one of advocacy of selective preferences, say in favor of Latin America and excluding India, quite clearly India would prefer nondiscrimination over such preferences. The issue for India is not really preferences or no preferences; vis-à-vis the United States, it is general preferences or nondiscrimination, even if the Indians have not phrased it quite that way."[11]

Thus, the G-77 approached UNCTAD I in an exceptionally poor position to negotiate with developed countries. Their positions were rigid because of the large number of compromises they already contained. Furthermore, because the negotiations were in a public forum, their inflexibility was increased by the need for solidarity among the G-77 and their desire not to appear to either their peers or their domestic audiences as acquiescing to the demands of the developed countries. In effect, the G-77 approached the UNCTAD I negotiations practically unable to negotiate. According to one of the observers:

The LDCs at the first UNCTAD Conference in 1964, committed to the notion that only unanimity would provide sufficient leverage, caucused together to develop a common position on the issues. Split in every conceivable way, the "Group of 77" could remain unified only by producing "maximum common denominator" positions. Compromise was difficult because any indication of flexibility threatened to unravel the unity the LDCs so desperately sought. Consequently, the "we" versus "they" confrontation was doubly disabling: It lent an unhappy appearance of extremism versus extremism to the negotiations, although many countries in both groups shared important views and positions, and made it easier to reject reasonable demands that were mixed in with, and often obscured by, ideological posturing.[12]

For a number of reasons, the United States was equally ill prepared to negotiate on the issues on the UNCTAD agenda. The United States had long been skeptical of commodity agreements and was virtually the only developed country that had strongly opposed preferential trading schemes in the past. U.S. positions on commodity agreements prior to UNCTAD have already been discussed. In regard to preferences, the United States had long supported nondiscrimination in international trade, opposing special trade concessions for individual countries. (U.S. officials had not forgotten the extensive use of such concessions by the German government in the interwar years, which not only caused disruption in international trade but also increased the vulnerability of benefiting countries to German pressures for political advantage.) Washington had stated its opposition to preferences early in the postwar period, during the negotiations on the International Trade Organization in 1947. However, as with many of the principles propounded by governments, this one was compromised by long-existing U.S. preferences for certain imports from the Philippines, and new preferences established for the Pacific islands formerly under Japanese control that the United States had begun to administer under the UN Trusteeship system (i.e., the Marshall, Caroline, and Marianas islands). In 1948, the United States requested from GATT a waiver of its nondiscrimination requirements for its preferences for these islands. This request was granted, but not before other GATT members worried aloud about the precedent being set.

However, by the time of UNCTAD I, trade and development issues were far from the major international economic issues for the United States. The attention of U.S. trade policy officials was focused on the Kennedy Round of tariff negotiations taking place under the auspices of the GATT. The Kennedy administration had a "grand design" in the field of international economic policy—the expansion of liberal free trade worldwide through a major reduction in the tariff levels of the EEC. The United States had strongly supported the creation of the EEC for political reasons, even though its discriminatory trade practices and the increase in protection of member states' markets contradicted U.S. policies favoring nondiscriminatory trade and reductions in barriers to trade. In the Kennedy Round of tariff negotiations, a key element in this grand design, the United States was pressing for a linear, 50 percent reduction in import duties by major trading nations.[13] The Kennedy Round began in May 1964 and was expected to continue until 1967. Anything that threatened to distract GATT members from negotiating seriously in the Kennedy Round was resisted in Washington.

The U.S. delegation to UNCTAD I was to be headed by George Ball, under secretary of state for economic affairs, who was a tough, blunt-spoken lawyer, strongly supportive of a liberal free-trading system, deeply involved in preparations for the Kennedy Round negotiations, and generally most interested in relations between the United States and its allies in Europe. His interest in the Third World was known to be limited.

On economic issues, Under Secretary Ball acted and sounded more like a typical official from the U.S. Treasury Department than one from the Department of State, taking a hard line against international economic proposals that did not fit into a liberal free-trade framework or that required expanded government management of international markets. He did not share the sympathies of many of his colleagues at the Department of State, particularly in the regional bureaus, who were more willing to factor in political considerations in formulating U.S. positions on North-South issues.

In his memoirs, Ball described his approach to UNCTAD I:

I would formally head the American delegation and make the initial American address on March 25. What, then, should I say? Veterans of such international conferences urged me to employ the traditional sympathetic waffle, and my colleagues in the State Department and the White House were horrified when I announced that I intended to make an honest, realistic statement to the conference. America, they argued, must never appear negative and indifferent to the aspirations of Third World nations; if we took an honest stance, other nations would take advantage of our forthrightness with empty promises.

I was aware that the delegates expected the United States to offer . . . generous-sounding promises. But I held to my commitment to candor. As I had expected, the speech fell like cold rain, but I am sure that the realism I injected at the outset saved the conference from even more absurd and unachievable recommendations than was finally the case.[14]

Interestingly enough, one area where the United States was apparently prepared to be supportive—that of creating a new organization to deal with trade and development issues—was not mentioned in Ball's speech. But an earlier speech by the assistant secretary of state for economic affairs, G. Griffith Johnson, had already signaled the U.S. position on this issue:

The Conference is likely to seek some technique whereby all aspects of trade and development, particularly as they relate to the problems of the less developed countries, can be viewed as a whole in a worldwide forum, and thus there is likely to be some reorganization of existing UN machinery to accomplish this purpose. We shall cooperate in seeking such a useful reorganization, recognizing the vital importance of preserving the integrity and autonomy of such organizations as the GATT and of preserving a sound and manageable structure within the UN.[15]

Thus, the United States went to UNCTAD I with positions that were opposed to nearly all of those supported by the G-77, with a chief of delegation whose interest in Third World issues was limited and who was strongly committed to ensuring that the upcoming Kennedy Round of tariff negotiations in GATT was a success. The only position on which the United States was prepared to be flexible was on the creation of a new international institution to deal with trade and development. This position had already in effect been conceded in a speech that Assistant Secretary Johnson had made before UNCTAD I began. And although the United States may have consulted with other developed countries, there is no evidence that an effort was made to develop coordinated positions on UNCTAD issues.

Indeed, among the developed countries, the diversity of positions, particularly on the key issue of preferences, was obvious. The UK was prepared to support generalized preferences if other developed countries also agreed, if the Commonwealth countries now enjoying preferential access to the British market agreed, and if generalized preferences were created through a lowering of tariffs for LDCs rather than an increase in tariffs on exports from other developed countries. Australia (which benefited from preferential access to the UK market) was prepared to introduce its own preferential scheme for LDCs. And Japan and Denmark had already implemented their own schemes of generalized preferences. The EEC had continued its preferences for Associated Overseas Territories as they gained their independence. The Soviets and other Socialist countries were supportive of preferences, but developing and developed countries alike recognized their support was meaningless, as tariff preferences had little significance in countries where trade was determined entirely by government fiat.

UNCTAD I, it is generally agreed, proved to be more a confrontation between North and South than a negotiation. The United States came with very little to offer the G-77 and offered little. Without U.S. active engagement in negotiating, little in the way of meaningful compromises was possible on the issues raised. The G-77 were unable or unwilling to negotiate either. In the words of one observer, they "would make uncompromising demands on what the UN calls the market economies, i.e., the Western industrialized countries, and would not only reject the latter's attempts at modification, but would even express dissatisfaction when demands were not accepted precisely as made."[16]

Issues at UNCTAD I were not negotiated among contending parties but were "resolved" through voting on resolutions. And the G-77 had the majority of votes, if not the financial and economic power to implement the resolutions. By sticking together, they were able to roll up large majorities on each resolution. The United States and other countries were left to express their opposition to such resolutions by voting against them. They had no obligation to implement resolutions they did not support.

A final comment on the significance of the nonnegotiation that UNCTAD I proved to be was made by Sidney Weintraub. It was, in his view, a "North-South confrontation, of the rich against the poor. There has been much talk in recent years that the division of the world, if one can talk of such a thing, should be along North-South economic lines rather than East-West lines of the cold war. UNCTAD was the first major conference where this was in fact the case."[17]

DISCUSSION QUESTIONS

1. *What was the U.S. negotiating position at UNCTAD I? What alternative strategies could the United States have pursued?*
2. *What was the impact of George Ball on the conference? Did his style and approach further U.S. interests?*
3. *Did the Group of 77 have any leverage in relation to the developed countries? How did the asymmetry between the blocs affect the multilateral negotiations?*
4. *How effective was the Group of 77 as a negotiating bloc?*

NOTES

1. Isaiah Frank, "Issues Before the UN Conference," *Foreign Affairs* (January 1964), 210.

2. J. C. Mills, "Canada at UNCTAD," *International Journal* (Spring 1965), 214.

3. Harry G. Johnson, *Economic Policies Toward Less Developed Countries* (New York: Praeger, 1967), 7.

4. U.S. House of Representatives, Subcommittee on Foreign Operations of the Appropriations Committee, *Hearings*, Mutual Security Appropriations for 1959 (Washington, D.C., 1958), 1336.

5. Clair Wilcox, Department of State official, *Hearings*, 1316.

6. Department of State *Bulletin* (April 8, 1963), 514.

7. Andrew Sholfield, "Trade as a Tool of Development," *International Affairs* (RIIA, April 1964), 219.

8. See Gardner Patterson, "Would Tariff Preferences Help Economic Development?" *Lloyds Bank Review* (April 1965).

9. Johnson, *Economic Policies*, chap. 6.

10. Since the beginning of the 1960s, GATT had begun to show much greater interest in trade and development issues. The contracting parties had endorsed a Program of Action for LDCs in May 1963, which included a standstill on any new tariff or nontariff barriers by developed countries against

the exports of LDCs; elimination of quantitative restrictions against imports from LDCs; duty-free entry for tropical products; elimination of tariffs on primary products; and reduction and elimination of tariff barriers to exports of semiprocessed products from LDCs by 50 percent over the coming three years. It was also decided to set up a working group to study the granting of preferences on selected products by industrialized countries.

11. Sidney Weintraub, *Trade Preferences for Less Developed Countries* (New York: Praeger, 1965).

12. Robert Rothstein, *The Weak in the World of the Strong* (New York: Columbia University Press, 1977), 147.

13. Gardner Patterson, *Discrimination in International Trade: The Policy Issues* (Princeton: Princeton University Press, 1966).

14. George Ball, *The Past Has Another Pattern* (New York: Norton, 1982), 194.

15. G. Griffith Johnson, "A Perspective on the United Nations Conference on Trade and Development," speech given before the tenth annual conference on international affairs sponsored by the Cincinnati Council on World Affairs, February 21, 1964. Printed in the Department of State *Bulletin* (March 16, 1964), 413.

16. Weintraub, *Trade Preferences*, 48.

17. *Ibid.*, 40.

FURTHER READING

Books

Ball, George. *The Past Has Another Pattern*. New York: W. W. Norton & Co., 1982.

Johnson, Harry G. *Economic Policies Toward Less Developed Countries*. New York: Praeger, 1967.

Rothstein, Robert. *The Weak in the World of the Strong*. New York: Columbia University Press, 1977.

Weintraub, Sidney. *Trade Preferences for Less Developed Countries*. New York: Praeger, 1965.

Weiss, Thomas G. *Multilateral Development Diplomacy in UNCTAD*. London: Macmillan, 1986.

Articles

Frank, Isaiah. "Issues Before the UN Conference." *Foreign Affairs* (January 1964): 210-226.

5

■ ══ ■

NEGOTIATING THE MONTREAL OZONE PROTOCOL

This chapter discusses the negotiations that led to the diplomatic conference in Montreal, in September 1987, at which an international protocol on substances that deplete the ozone layer was concluded. It is an example of a *medium-sized* multi-lateral negotiation. The subject of this case study is the *environment*, which is gaining increasing priority on the international diplomatic agenda, and which will be the focus of more multilateral negotiations in the future. The case illustrates that negotiators must be sensitive to their different domestic constituencies in order to secure agreements that will be accepted. It stresses the crucial role an *international organization or specialized agency*, in this case the United Nations Environmental Program, can play in the negotiating process.

DECIDING TO NEGOTIATE

The Case for an International Agreement to Protect the Ozone Layer

What scientists today refer to as the ozone layer is a region approximately 10 kilometers (km) wide in the part of the earth's upper atmosphere called the

---

This chapter is an edited version of the case study by Allan E. Goodman, The Negotiations Leading to the 1987 Montreal Protocol on Substances That Deplete the Ozone Layer, *Pew case study no. 447.*

stratosphere. In this region, the concentration of ozone—a pale blue gas formed from the effect of electrical discharges (e.g., lightning) on oxygen—is some 10 parts per million (ppm), compared to 0.04 ppm in the part of the atmosphere that we breathe, the troposphere. And at this level of concentration (which, if it were compressed to that of air pressure on the earth's surface, would be less than one-eighth of an inch thick), ozone in the stratosphere absorbs 99 percent of the ultraviolet radiation from the sun. Hence, without this small ozone layer, Earth would be effectively sterilized and devoid of life as we know it.

Apparently, to the extent that ozone is depleted—a process that will be described below—more of the sun's harmful ultraviolet radiation will reach the earth's surface. Dermatologists have long believed that enhanced ultraviolet radiation is directly related to the incidence of skin cancer, now said to be at epidemic proportions in the United States, where more than half a million new cases are reported each year, and rapidly increasing in other countries.[1] Working together with atmospheric scientists, physicians have developed a "rule of thumb . . . that if you had an 'x' percent drop in ozone you might expect about a two or three times 'x' percent increase in skin cancer assuming that living styles remain constant."[2] Scientists now calculate that for even very small (e.g., 1 percent) decreases in ozone in the stratosphere, thousands of people are more likely to develop skin cancer and other diseases caused by the effects of ultraviolet radiation on human life. Such increases in radiation would also affect plant and animal life, although there has been insufficient testing to determine which species would be most deleteriously affected.

Ozone atoms are broken down entirely by atmospheric pollutants created by humans, and concern about depletion of the ozone layer is not new. In the early 1970s, for example, when the U.S. and other governments were considering development of supersonic transport (SST) aircraft that would fly within the ozone layer in the stratosphere, scientists discovered that the nitric oxide (NO) produced by the aircraft's jet engines reduced ozone to oxygen. And in 1974, the Climatic Impact Assessment Program of the U.S. Department of Transportation concluded that a fleet of about 500 SSTs operating seven to eight hours per day would cause a 15 percent depletion of the ozone layer in the Northern Hemisphere and an 8 percent depletion in the Southern Hemisphere. However, by the time the two Concorde SSTs became operational, engineers had designed the craft to fly at much lower altitudes than these calculations assumed, and hence, they pose almost no threat to the ozone layer today.

Another early source of concern was the effect of the U.S. space shuttle. The solid-fuel rocket boosters used to launch the shuttle release hydrogen chloride (HCl) as they burn, and at the rate of one launch per week (the schedule projected for the shuttle in 1972, when the decision to use solid fuel rockets was made by National Aeronautics and Space Administration—NASA) environmental scientists estimated that more than 5,000 tons of HCl would be released into the stratosphere annually. Eventually, in 1977, the scientists concluded that even this amount of HCl would only result in a reduction of the ozone somewhere in the range of 0.07 to 0.6 percent. Rocket and environmental scientists later discovered that in addition to HCl, each time a shuttle is launched, 20 tons of CFC-113 is released into the stratosphere; as will be discussed below, this poses a much greater threat to the ozone layer.

Ozone depletion also emerged as an international public policy issue in the mid-1970s largely as a result of U.S. government statements and actions. In 1975, ozone depletion was discussed at a NATO conference at the insistence of the U.S. Environmental Protection Agency. In the wake of the passage of the 1977 ozone protection amendment to the Clean Air Act and the banning of use of chlorofluorocarbons (CFCs) in most domestic aerosol products in 1978, U.S. environmental officials and experts began to press for similar actions by other governments. Also in 1977, the countries then participating in a series of ongoing discussions under the auspices of the United Nations Environment Program (UNEP) developed a plan of action that among other things, called for the establishment of a Coordinating Committee on the Ozone Layer (CCOL) to undertake annual reviews of the relevant scientific information and atmospheric developments. A decade later there was a meeting to negotiate an international agreement for the protection of the ozone layer and the reduction of CFC emissions.

By far the most substantial threat to the ozone layer comes from the release of CFCs. They were first developed in the 1930s by General Motors as a replacement for ammonia in the refrigeration industry. But because CFCs proved nontoxic, inert, and easy to liquify, they were soon used in a variety of industries. By 1986, "the annual value of goods and services which [depended] to a varying extent upon CFCs [exceeded] $28 billion, and more than 780,000 full-time jobs [were] related to CFC uses in the United States."[3] By 1987, when limits on future CFC production appeared likely to be part of the Montreal Protocol, the U.S. Department of Commerce estimated that more than 400 industrial sectors would be adversely affected.

Between 1963 and 1975, total worldwide production of CFCs increased from some 500 million pounds to 2 billion pounds annually. For the next nine years, annual production fell to between 1.6 and 1.8 billion pounds owing to U.S. government regulations banning the use of CFCs as an aerosol propellant. In 1984, as other countries developed their own CFC industries, annual production rose above the 2 billion pound level and has steadily increased.

Because CFCs are inert and very stable, they are not affected by other chemicals in or the dynamics of the lower Earth atmosphere. Hence, they percolate up through the troposphere into the stratosphere, where they are broken down by the sun's ultraviolet radiation into chlorine atoms, which in turn decompose ozone (back into oxygen) and regenerate a new chlorine atom that goes off in search of more ozone to decompose. Sunlight also decomposes ozone naturally, but the result is oxygen, not chlorine. The abundance of oxygen that is constantly being created makes it possible for additional ozone to be formed by the reactions described at the beginning of this case study, but as a result of CFC emissions, one chlorine atom can go on to destroy 100,000 ozone molecules. Eventually, "the chlorine atom that was delivered to the stratosphere [by CFC emissions] . . . returns to the lower atmosphere as hydrochloric acid in rain. . . . That entire cycle takes about a hundred years on the average."[4]

The most widely used CFCs (CFC-11 and CFC-12) not only have the highest apparent ozone depletion capability but also have an estimated lifetime in the stratosphere of 63.8 and 107.8 years respectively. Other less widely used CFCs have a lifetime estimated to range from 27.7 years (for CFC-22) to 88 years (for CFC-113 released as a result of space shuttle launches) to 385.3 years (for CFC-115).[5] Thus, even if all CFC emissions were immediately halted—something the Montreal Protocol does not call for—scientists estimate that the natural predatory effect of the chlorine atoms already present in the stratosphere because of CFC emissions to date will result in a significant depletion of the ozone layer globally by the year 2050.

For some regions, the depletion effect appears to be occurring much more rapidly, as was dramatically revealed by the discovery in 1985 of a "large, sudden and unanticipated decrease in the abundance of springtime Antarctic ozone over the last decade."[6] Visually, this decrease appeared to create a hole over much of the subcontinent. In addition, a report based on data collected by the Nimbus-7 weather satellite, also issued in 1985, indicated that there had been decreases on a global scale of the total ozone layer of about 1 percent per year and of about 3 percent per year at the 50 km altitude. This report was not so alarming as the data initially appeared to suggest, however. Some scientists were critical of the method by which the data was collected. Other scientists and most policymakers, moreover, were not yet convinced that ozone depletion at these levels was necessarily harmful to human life or could be linked to the increased incidence of skin cancer because that disease takes many years of sun damage to manifest itself.

What caught the attention of policymakers was the Antarctic hole. It was about the size of the United States and as deep as the height of Mount Everest, and it appeared when the chlorine level in the stratosphere above Antarctica reached a level of just three parts per billion.

The Position of the CFC Industry

Although the need for effective international action to protect the ozone layer was a well-established precept in environmentalist circles and the need for urgency was dramatized by the satellite photograph of the Antarctic hole, there was no scientific or governmental consensus in 1985 and 1986 on what was causing the ozone depletion or how the apparent trends mentioned above could best be reversed or, at least, halted. Even as late as March 1987, some U.S. government scientists maintained, as one from NASA did in testimony before the Subcommittee on Health and the Environment of the House of Representatives Commerce Committee, that "the cause of the recently observed Antarctic ozone hole is not yet understood . . . If the hole is shown to be caused by CFCs in a mechanism that would destroy ozone on a global scale, then the need for CFC regulation would be significantly enhanced. For the present, however, I consider the Antarctic hole to be an indication that the ozone layer is indeed fragile, and subject to significant modification."[7] It is hardly surprising, therefore, that throughout 1985 and 1986 the CFC industries in the United States and other countries were opposed to the regulation of their activities, especially as a result of intergovernmental negotiations and a process of multilateral diplomacy that involved UN agencies and the intense Third World politicking that had come to characterize the secretariats of those agencies.

In the United States, CFC manufacturers and users were represented by a lobbying organization known as the Alliance for Responsible CFC Policy, which was formed in 1980. By late fall 1986, the alliance had taken a clear and strong stand against "premature regulation" and through its chairman, Richard Barnett, made the following points:

- There is ample time to develop effective solutions to address . . . concerns [about ozone depletion], but they will require a global focus and the cooperative efforts of industry and government . . .
- We should not rush into short-term regulatory decisions that could result in the use of alternatives that present immediate threats to worker and consumer safety and offer little or no environmental benefit . . .
- In general, the Alliance does not believe that the scientific information demonstrates any actual risk from current CFC use or emissions. We recognize, however, the growing concern for potential ozone depletion and climate change in the future as a result of large continuing growth of CFC emissions and the buildup of many other trace gases in the atmosphere, and the concern generated by the discovery of unexplained phenomena such as the large reductions in ozone levels during the Antarctic spring
- On the basis of current information, we believe that large future increases in fully halogenated CFCs (the most durable ones, thought to contribute most to ozone depletion) would be unacceptable to future generations. . . . In furtherance of this position, the Alliance recently issued a policy statement which included support for a negotiated global limit on the future rate of

growth of fully halogenated CFC production capacity; the development of voluntary programs by industries to conserve CFCs and
reduce CFC emissions; and the continuation of research to develop
acceptable substitutes for the fully halogenated CFCs.[8]

Throughout the intragovernmental and international negotiations in 1986
and 1987 that led up to the Montreal Protocol, the alliance also tried to
publicize the likely cost to the U.S. consumer of capping or banning CFC
production or use. Toward this end, the alliance contracted with a prestigious
energy-consulting firm, Putnam, Hayes & Bartlett (PHB), to develop a range
of estimates of the costs of regulating CFCs based on the types of
limits—domestic and international—then under discussion. The PHB study
forecasts substantial economic dislocation when such regulations would come
into force, ranging from CFC price increases two-to-four times greater than
those prevailing in 1986 to declines in the performance and quality of some
electronic parts to the elimination of some packaging businesses altogether
(e.g., if egg cartons made with CFC substitutes became more expensive than
their contents).[9] Hence, the goal of the alliance throughout the period
covered by this case was "to prevent any unproductive, harmful, unwarranted
unilateral domestic regulatory program that would injure US industry to the
benefit of our international competition."[10]

Private industry, speaking through the alliance, was concerned that no
international agreement be predicated on or require domestic regulations
thought to be unfair or unwise and sought to involve itself in both the international as well as the domestic negotiations over CFC regulations and
production limits. It is not unusual for U.S. industries to become deeply
involved in framing the U.S. position toward international negotiations that
affect corporate profits and jobs. In fact, the Congress mandates that the
private sector be consulted by the State and Commerce departments and the
Office of the Special Trade Representative on most international trade
negotiations. U.S. negotiators ignore the concerns of private industry only at
their peril, for if an agreement is negotiated that industry cannot support or
on which its lobby groups were not at least asked to submit their views, the
risk is very great that Congress will not ratify the agreement or will seek to
change what has been negotiated by adding new demands, insisting that negotiations be reopened, or holding departmental appropriations hostage to
changes in the U.S. position.

The U.S. Position

The responsibility for framing the official U.S. government position
belonged to the State Department and the Environmental Protection Agency
(EPA). They were assisted by several other government agencies, which

provided scientific and technical expertise.[11]   By the fall of 1986, these agencies had reached consensus on a draft statement, "Circular 175," which contained the principles of the U.S. position that were to be followed during negotiations and a draft protocol text. The principles agreed upon were the following:

1. A near-term freeze on the combined emissions of the most ozone-depleting substances;
2. A long-term scheduled reduction of emissions of these chemicals down to the point of eliminating emissions from all but limited uses for which no substitutes are commercially available (such reduction could be as much as 95 percent), subject to 3; and
3. Periodic reviews of the protocol provisions based upon regular assessment of the science. The review could remove or add chemicals, or change the schedule or the emission reduction target.[12]

DISCUSSION QUESTIONS

1. *As the U.S. representative, you are expected to negotiate with Chairman Barnett and to gain alliance support and approval of the principles adopted for negotiations. What is your negotiating strategy?*
2. *How would you respond to Barnett's concern about the costs of premature or unilateral regulation? How would you deal with the lack of hard scientific evidence on the causes of ozone depletion over Antarctica in the spring and uncertainty about the accuracy of measurements indicating a global decline in ozone?*
3. *What tactics will Barnett likely use to ensure that the proposed protocol conforms to the alliance position? What countermeasures can you employ?*
4. *How can you best keep the White House informed and supportive of the State Department, knowing that the alliance has access to high officials on the president's staff as well as to the secretaries of commerce and energy and the administrator of the Environmental Protection Agency?*

REACHING AN AGREEMENT

The Role of UNEP

Concern about developing a protocol on the ozone layer was not occurring in a vacuum. The United Nations Environment Program, with headquarters in Nairobi, played an important role in publicizing the dangers from ozone depletion and laying the groundwork for measures to protect the ozone layer. Under its indefatigable director, Mostafa Tolba, an Egyptian scientist, it organized conferences and symposia to discuss ozone depletion. In 1981 UNEP established an ad hoc working group of technical and legal experts to draft a convention and a separate protocol on the ozone layer.

In March 1985, forty-three countries concluded an ozone convention in Vienna, which was "a considerable accomplishment. It represented the first effort of the international community formally to deal with an environmental danger before it erupted."[13] However, although the convention obligated signatories to take measures to protect the ozone layer, such measures remained unspecified. Furthermore, there was a conspicuous absence of any reference to specific chemicals that deplete the ozone layer.

Nevertheless, UNEP was asked to continue its efforts at securing a legally binding protocol. It organized two preparatory workshops: the first, sponsored by the European Community, was held in Rome in May 1986, and the second, sponsored by the United States, was held in Leesburg, Virginia, in September of that year. The objective was to get delegates from the main countries participating in the UNEP negotiations to discuss their conceptual differences without having to resolve them or formally represent and defend national and industry positions. The Rome workshop was characterized by much dissension, especially over future CFC production and consumption trends. The Leesburg workshop was more congenial, and the most significant development was the decision that an "interim protocol" would be drafted that could be revised in light of new scientific knowledge. This would allow governments to take steps to protect the ozone layer without "a definitive solution to the CFC problem."[14]

The Draft and Positions

At a meeting of the UNEP held in Geneva in December 1986, the United States submitted the following draft treaty on protecting the ozone layer:

United States Draft Protocol Text
UNEP Negotiations on an Ozone Layer Protocol

December 1-5, 1986
Geneva, Switzerland

The United States believes that the potential risks to the stratospheric ozone layer from certain man-made chemicals require early and concerted action by the international community. Since the adoption in Vienna in March 1985 of the Ozone Layer Convention, an intensive scientific research and technical analysis effort has been carried out and is continuing, as reflected in the recent series of UNEP-Sponsored workshops. The results continue to indicate the emergence of a serious environmental problem of global proportions. . . .

In response to UNEP's invitation, the U.S. has prepared for discussion purposes a draft text based on the U.S. views statement which we recently circulated. This text is for the operative articles only, and is designed for incorporation into the protocol text developed during the previous round of negotiations (i.e., it would replace Articles II through V of the fourth revised draft text).

The United States believes that what is required is a straightforward, cost-effective approach that will provide technology incentives and clear targets to governments and industry for developing and introducing new technologies for chemical conservation, recycling and substitution. The U.S. believes that its proposed text provides such an approach.

U.S. Draft Protocol Text: Operative Articles

Article II: Control Measures

1. Within [] years after entry into force of this Protocol, each Party shall ensure that its aggregate annual emissions of fully-halogenated alkanes does not exceed its 1986 level.
2. Within [] years after entry into force of this Protocol, each Party shall ensure that its aggregate annual emissions of fully-halogenated alkanes is reduced by [20] percent from its 1986 level.
3. Within [] years after entry into force of this Protocol, each Party shall ensure that its aggregate annual emissions of fully-halogenated alkanes is reduced by [50] percent from its 1986 level.
4. Within [] years after entry into force of this Protocol, each Party shall ensure that its aggregate annual emissions of fully-halogenated alkanes is reduced by [95] percent from its 1986 level.
5. The right of any Party to adopt control measures more stringent than contained herein is not restricted by this Article.

Article III: Calculation of Aggregate Annual Emissions

1. For the purposes of Article II, each Party shall calculate its aggregate annual emissions by taking its:
   a. aggregate annual production;
   [b. plus aggregate annual bulk imports;]
   [c. minus aggregate annual bulk exports to other Parties;]

[d. minus aggregate annual amount of fully-halogenated alkanes which have been destroyed or permanently encapsulated.]
2. To calculate the aggregate amounts specified in the subparagraphs of paragraph 1, each Party shall multiply the amount of each fully-halogenated alkane by its ozone depletion weight, as specified in Annex A, and then add the products.

Article IV: Assessment and Adjustment of Control Measures

1. The Parties shall cooperate in establishing an international monitoring network for detecting, or aiding in the prediction of modification of the ozone layer.
2. At least one year before implementing the reductions specified in paragraphs 2, 3, and 4, respectively, of Article II, the Parties shall convene an ad hoc panel of scientific experts, with composition and terms of reference determined by the Parties, to review advances in scientific understanding of modification of the ozone layer and the potential health, environmental, and climatic effects of such modification.
3. In light of such scientific review, the Parties shall jointly assess and may adjust the stringency, timing, and scope of the control measures in Article II and the ozone depletion weights in Annex A.
4. Any such adjustment shall be made by amending Article II and/or Annex A as provided in Article 9 of the Convention, except that such amendment would not be subject to the six month advance notice requirement of paragraph 2 of that Article.

Article V: Control of Trade

1. Within [] years after entry into force of this Protocol, each Party shall ban the import of fully-halogenated alkanes in bulk from any state not party to this Protocol [, unless such state is in full compliance with Article II and this Article and has submitted information to that effect as specified in paragraph 1 of Article VI].
2. Within [] years after entry into force of this Protocol, each Party shall ban:
   a. the export of technologies to the territory of non-parties
   [b. direct investment in facilities in the territory of non-parties] for producing fully-halogenated alkanes [, unless such state is in full compliance with Article II and this

Article and has submitted information to that effect as specified in paragraph 1 of Article VI].

3. The Parties shall jointly study the feasibility of restricting imports of products containing or produced with fully-halogenated alkanes from any state not party to this Protocol.

Article VI: Reporting of Information

1. Each Party shall submit annually to the Secretariat data showing its calculation of aggregate annual emissions of fully-halogenated alkanes, as specified in Article III, using the format developed by the Secretariat pursuant to paragraph 3a.

2. Each party shall submit to the Secretariat appropriate information to indicate its compliance with Article V.

3. The Secretariat shall:
   a. develop and distribute to all Parties a standard format for reporting such data as indicated by paragraph 1;
   b. take appropriate measures to ensure the confidentiality of all data submitted to it pursuant to paragraph 1, except for the aggregate annual emissions figures;
   c. compile and distribute annually to all Parties a report of the aggregate annual emissions figures and other information submitted to it pursuant to paragraph 2.

The negotiations at Geneva lasted a week. Participating were twenty-five countries, including nineteen industrialized and six developing countries. There were three main negotiating blocs at Geneva. The first was the European Community (EC), which strongly supported the position of industry, and whose negotiating position was influenced by France, Italy, and the United Kingdom. The EC also had Japan and the Soviet Union as allies. The EC Commission maintained that there should be a cap on production, that reductions in production should be postponed, that substituting chlorofluorocarbons in aerosols would affect their quality, and that there were no readily available alternatives to fluorocarbon.[15]

The second bloc consisted of Canada, Finland, New Zealand, Norway, Sweden, Switzerland, and the United States. These countries supported strong measures, arguing that the production of CFCs would continue to have adverse effects on the atmosphere and that delaying constructive action would lead to grave consequences. Although they were aware that the scientific evidence was not comprehensive or foolproof, they believed that enough was known to warrant effective measures being taken.

The third bloc was composed of Australia, Austria, and several developing countries, including Argentina, Brazil, Egypt, and Kenya. At the outset of negotiations they maintained a neutral stance on the key issues. However, as negotiations progressed, they supported the adoption of strong controls.[16]

DISCUSSION QUESTIONS

With the members of the class divided into the three negotiating blocs described above, representatives of each group might be asked to give brief presentations covering the following questions:

1. *From the perspective of your bloc, what problems do you have with the U.S. draft text?*
2. *What is the purpose of the proposals in Article V to restrict trade in controlled substances with nonparties?*
3. *What are the advantages and disadvantages of proposing an initial freeze rather than immediate cuts?*

ENDGAME

After the Geneva conference, the countries of the main negotiating blocs still disagreed on a number of issues. They were the following: chemical coverage; production versus consumption; the base year for determining future reductions; stringency and timing of reductions; the treaty's entry into force, revisions, and voting; trade restrictions with countries not party to the protocol; developing countries, which consume low levels of chlorofluorocarbons; and special provisions for the European Community.[17]

With regard to chemical coverage, the countries in the second bloc maintained that all substances that were known to cause significant depletion of the ozone layer should be covered by the protocol. In contrast, the European Community wanted only CFC-11 and CFC-12 controlled, and Japan opposed including CFC-113, as it was widely used in the Japanese electronics industry.

The blocs were also divided on whether restrictions should apply to the production or the consumption of controlled substances. Bloc two countries (and the Soviet Union) advocated the application of restrictions to consumption because they feared that focusing on production would favor producing countries, especially members of the European Community. Not surprisingly, bloc one (led by the European Community) supported the production formula. They argued that because only a limited number of countries produced the relevant substances, in contrast to a plethora of industries that used them, it would be easier and more effective to control production. Furthermore, the European Community was concerned that if the focus were on consumption, a reduction in U.S. domestic demand would encourage U.S. producers to expand into overseas markets that were dominated by European countries.

The most divisive issue was the stringency and timing of reductions. In the draft text the United States submitted for consideration at Geneva, it advocated a freeze in production followed by three successive reductions at 20 percent, 50 percent, and 95 percent of the base year. The European Community, however, was firmly committed to a continued increase in production.

As the delegates to the UNEP plenary meeting in Vienna convened for negotiations in February 1987, the U.S. delegate, Ambassador Richard E. Benedick, prepared a statement that was critical of the industrialized countries, including Britain, France, Japan, and the Soviet Union. He accused them of seeking delays and favoring only a modest and weak agreement so that their domestic chemical industries would be protected and possibly even gain an advantage over U.S. industry if Congress imposed further CFC production and use limits by amending the Clear Air Act. The statement was also intended to be critical of the so-called newly industrialized countries (e.g., South Korea, India) that wished to establish, or greatly expand, CFC industries in order to reap profits by producing CFCs banned in the United States. As Ambassador Benedick noted, there was "widening informal agreement on many aspects of a protocol, including a near-term freeze and longer term reductions. . . . But the hardest negotiations are still to come. The participants must still negotiate the specific stringency and timing of controls, determine precisely which substances are to be restricted, and specify treatment of developing countries, nonparties, and late-signers."[18]

The negotiating countries, which by this time numbered thirty-three returned to Geneva in April 1987 for further negotiations. This was the first session attended by Mostafa Tolba, UNEP's executive director, and he played a crucial role in discussions. Employing the methods of informal diplomacy, he organized a series of meetings of the heads of the most important delegations (Belgium, Canada, Denmark, Japan, New Zealand, Norway, the Soviet Union, the United Kingdom, the United States, and the EC Commission), to draft an informal text. As work progressed on the draft, it bore close resemblance to that submitted by the United States in Geneva four months before. Significant advance was made on the most divisive issue, namely, the size and timing of reductions: The Tolba text provided for a freeze within two years after the protocol entered into force, followed by a 20 percent reduction four years later. Nevertheless, not all the countries agreed to this formula, and Tolba convened another meeting in Brussels at the end of June to resolve outstanding differences. That summer the United States engaged in intense international diplomacy in order to garner support for its position. Its embassies used public diplomacy to keep other governments informed of unresolved issues and to win them over.

The Montreal conference opened on September 8 with sixty countries in attendance, as well as representatives of various environmental groups and industrial organizations. Working groups were established to gain consensus on the remaining issues, and Tolba and Winfried Lang of Austria, the conference chairman, had several closed meetings with delegation heads to gain agreement. After eight days of intense negotiations, mostly conducted away from the glare of publicity, the protocol was completed and signed by twenty-four countries and the European Commission.

DISCUSSION QUESTIONS

1. *What would you advise Ambassador Benedick to do to ameliorate the negative reactions to his statement, especially those of some European and Asian delegates?*
2. *How would you deal with these issues: stringency and timing of controls? production versus consumption? substances to be restricted? treatment of developing countries?*
3. *What impact did a nonstate actor such as UNEP have on the negotiating process? the EC Commission?*

NOTES

1. Medwin M. Mintzis, "Skin Cancer: The Price for a Depleted Ozone Layer," *EPA Journal* (December 1986), 7.

2. Interview with Michael McElroy, *Harvard Alumni Gazette* (June 1988), 34. McElroy is a professor of atmospheric science at Harvard University and one of the discoverers of the loss of Antarctic ozone.

3. Richard Barnett, "Ozone Protection: The Need for a Global Solution," *EPA Journal* (December 1986), 10.

4. McElroy interview.

5. Donald J. Wuebbles, "Chlorocarbon Emissions Scenarios: Potential Impact on Stratospheric Ozone," *Journal of Geophysical Research* 88 (February 20, 1983), 1433-1443.

6. Executive Summary of Ozone Trends Panel, Press Conference, National Aeronautics and Space Administration Headquarters, Washington, D.C., March 15, 1988, 1.

7. Statement of Robert T. Watson, Earth Science and Applications Division, Office of Space Science and Applications, National Aeronautics and Space Administration, March 5, 1987, 8.

8. Barnett, "Ozone Protection," 10-11. The halogens—chlorine, fluorine, bromine, and iodine—all react with hydrogen to help in the process of forming gaseous compounds.

9. The PHB study findings are cited in David E. Gushee, "Clean Air Act: Protection of the Stratospheric Ozone Layer," *Congressional Research Service Issue Brief* (March 1, 1988), 8.

10. Barnett, "Ozone Protection," 10.

11. See Richard Elliot Benedick, *Ozone Diplomacy: New Directions in Safeguarding the Planet* (Cambridge, Mass.: Harvard University Press, 1991), 50-53.

12. *Ibid.*, 53.

13. *Ibid.*, 45.

14. *Ibid.*, 49-50.

15. See *ibid.*, 68-69.

16. *Ibid.*, 69.

17. This section is based on *ibid.*, 77-97.

18. Richard E. Benedick, Address to the Washington Conference on CFCs, March 25, 1987, reprinted in *International Efforts to Protect the Stratospheric Ozone Layer* (United States Department of State, Bureau of Public Affairs, Current Policy No. 931), 3-4.

FURTHER READING

Books

Benedick, Richard Elliot. *Ozone Diplomacy: New Directions in Safeguarding the Planet*. Cambridge, Mass.: Harvard University Press, 1991.

Dotto, Lydia, and Harold Schiff. *The Ozone War*. Garden City, N.Y.: Doubleday, 1978.

Gribbin, John. *The Hole in the Sky*. New York: Bantam, 1988.

Haigh, Nigel. *EEC Environmental Policy and Britain*, 2d ed. London: Longman, 1989.

Articles

Jachtenfuchs, Markus. "The European Community and the Protection of the Ozone Layer." *Journal of Common Market Studies* 28, 3 (March 1990): 261-277.

Lammers, Johan G. "Efforts to Develop a Protocol on Chlorofluorocarbons to the Vienna Convention for the Protection of the Ozone Layer." *Hague Yearbook of International Law* 1 (1988): 225-269

Tripp, James T.B. "The UNEP Montreal Protocol: Industrialized and Developing Countries Sharing the Responsibility for Protecting the Stratospheric Ozone Layer." *Journal of International Law and Politics* 20, 3 (1988): 733-752.

6

NEGOTIATING A MINERALS REGIME FOR ANTARCTICA

This chapter focuses on the attempts of twenty countries to negotiate a minerals regime for Antarctica. It is an example of a *small* multilateral negotiation that focuses on natural resource issues. It examines the reasons for their decision to enter into negotiations, as well as the goals and strategies of the different countries. It reveals the problems associated with negotiations on important natural resources, which often involve contentious territorial claims and issues of sovereignty. It discusses the process of building consensus in multilateral negotiations and sheds light on this form of decisionmaking. Informal diplomacy was an important component of these negotiations, and its role in international diplomacy is emphasized. The case also demonstrates the influence of a *chairperson* on the conduct and outcome of negotiations.

DECIDING TO NEGOTIATE

Few people know that there exists a controversy about who, if anyone, owns Antarctica. For years, a small but influential group of countries has

This chapter is an edited version of the case study by William Westermeyer and Christopher Joyner, Negotiating a Minerals Regime for Antarctica, *Pew case study no. 134.*

been conducting scientific research in Antarctica. Research has shown that Antarctica, although largely covered by ice, is a normal continent in most respects and that, therefore, it may contain a considerable amount of *potentially* valuable minerals.

The possibility that minerals may be discovered in significant amounts in Antarctica and that someday they could be exploited is an important concern of countries active there because, in the absence of agreed sovereignty, it is not at all clear who, if anyone, owns the resources. In order to avoid possible conflicts over future resource exploitation and to provide a regulatory regime that balances development with scientific, environmental, and other objectives, countries active in Antarctica formally decided in 1981 to negotiate an agreement governing the exploitation of mineral resources. The resulting Convention on the Regulation of Antarctic Mineral Resource Activities (CRAMRA) was adopted in June 1988 and since then has been under consideration for ratification by the participating governments.

The countries involved in the mineral negotiations are all parties to the 1959 Antarctic Treaty, and it was within the context of the broader Antarctic Treaty System that negotiations were conducted. These countries included the twelve original signatories (Argentina, Australia, Belgium, Chile, France, Japan, New Zealand, Norway, South Africa, the Soviet Union, the United Kingdom, and the United States) and eight more-recent signatories (Brazil, the People's Republic of China, the Federal Republic of Germany, the German Democratic Republic, India, Italy, Poland, and Uruguay). These twenty countries constituted the group of Antarctic Treaty Consultative Parties (ATCPs) at the time of the final negotiating session. Their status as original treaty signatories and/or the fact that they currently conduct research in Antarctica distinguishes them from other treaty signatories. Notably, under the terms of the treaty, these attributes give them voting rights on all issues covered by the treaty.

To appreciate why the ATCPs decided in 1981 that the time had come to establish a minerals regime for Antarctica as quickly as possible, one must understand the history and development of the Antarctic Treaty System (ATS). The ATS is composed of various agreements made for governing activities of countries in Antarctica. The cornerstone and most important of these agreements is the Antarctic Treaty, which entered into force in 1961.

The Antarctic Treaty grew out of the success of the International Geophysical Year (IGY) of 1957-1958. The IGY was a program designed to promote global scientific cooperation. Antarctica was chosen as one of two foci of coordinated scientific research during this period. At the conclusion of the IGY, "many scientists and diplomats felt that the program in Antarctica was too valuable to terminate and that the international cooperation achieved during IGY should be maintained."[1] Accordingly, in 1959 the United States invited all those countries that had conducted scientific research in Antarctica during the period to Washington, D.C., to discuss the possibility of establishing a treaty.

The treaty that resulted from the Washington talks is generally considered to be a model example of international cooperation. Among the important provisions of the treaty are those that (1) provide that Antarctica shall be used for peaceful purposes only, thus limiting military activities south of sixty degrees south latitude to logistical support of scientific research; (2) institutionalize unrestricted access to Antarctica for scientific purposes; (3) prohibit nuclear explosions and the disposal of nuclear waste; (4) provide for the exchange of scientific data and personnel; and (5) enable signatories to inspect each other's research stations and other installations.[2]

The most difficult issue negotiators had to confront during the treaty talks was how to handle the problem of territorial claims. Seven of the original twelve countries active in Antarctica had previously made claims to portions of the continent. The other five countries neither had claims of their own nor recognized the claims of the others. Two of these countries, the United States and the Soviet Union, did contend that they also had legitimate reasons for making claims and reserved the right to do so in the future. To complicate the issue further, three of the existing claims (those of Argentina, Chile, and the United Kingdom) overlapped. No part of the Antarctic continent was clearly owned by any country. Recognizing that the claims issue could not be resolved easily and that other goals were mutually important, the negotiators circumvented the issue with an innovative solution, embodied in Article IV of the Antarctic Treaty.

Article IV, which has important implications for the minerals regime negotiations, provides in full:

1. Nothing contained in the present treaty shall be interpreted as:
   a renunciation by any Contracting Party of previously asserted rights of or claims to territorial sovereignty in Antarctica; (b) a renunciation or diminution by any Contracting Party of any basis of claim to territorial sovereignty in Antarctica which it may have whether as a result of its activities or those of its nationals in Antarctica, or otherwise; (c) prejudicing the position of any Contracting Party as regards its recognition or non-recognition of any other States rights of or claim or basis of claim to territorial sovereignty in Antarctica.
2. No acts or activities taking place while the present treaty is in force shall constitute a basis for asserting, supporting or denying a claim to territorial sovereignty in Antarctica or create any rights of sovereignty in Antarctica. No new claim, or enlargement of an existing claim, to territorial sovereignty in Antarctica shall be asserted while the present treaty is in force.[3]

The compromise embodied in Article IV enabled the ATCPs to establish a treaty which has proved to be very effective in promoting cooperation and the peaceful uses of Antarctica. At the same time, the compromise left the potentially divisive claims issue unresolved.

It has occasionally been pointed out that the treaty was a modest, limited, and relatively cost-free attempt at international control—essentially a formal version of the status quo reached during the IGY. The treaty is therefore significant for what it does not address. It makes no mention of and gives no guidance for the exploitation of either renewable, living resources within the treaty area (i.e., land, ice, and water areas south of sixty degrees south latitude) or of nonrenewable mineral resources. To have attempted to deal with resource issues would have gone well beyond the original goals of the treaty negotiators and, especially for nonliving resources, would have required that the claims issue be faced directly. Moreover, Antarctic resource exploitation was not considered feasible in 1959, and negotiators could not have foreseen that less than thirty years later states would be positioning themselves for possible mineral exploration and exploitation in Antarctica.[4]

The Antarctic Treaty System has grown in important ways since the Antarctica Treaty entered into force. The treaty provides for regular consultative party meetings, which have produced several consensus agreements (formally known as recommendations) on issues ranging from environmental protection to the regulation of tourism. On occasion, means other than recommendations have been used to respond to issues requiring common action. For example, the Agreed Measures for the Conservation of Antarctic Fauna and Flora were developed in recognition of the need to conserve the living resources of the treaty area. The Convention for the Conservation of Antarctic Seals established a management regime for hunting, if it should recommence in the treaty area. And the Convention on the Conservation of Antarctic Marine Living Resources (CCAMLR) established a management regime for the exploitation of all living resources in the circumpolar southern seas. CCAMLR, although negotiated as a separate, stand-alone agreement by the ATCPs, embodies the principles of the Antarctic Treaty.

CCAMLR, which entered into force in 1982, deserves special mention. The convention was not easy to negotiate, but its ultimate ratification by the ATCPs does suggest that negotiation of a regime governing the exploitation of minerals could be accomplished without undue difficulty. There are, however, important differences between living and nonliving resources. Most living resources are mobile (for example, the abundant Antarctic krill) and, therefore, not easily contained within the jurisdiction of any one country. Moreover, Article IV of the Antarctic Treaty recognizes the existence of high seas within the treaty area and declares that "nothing in the present Treaty shall prejudice or in any way affect the rights [one of which is the right to fish], or the exercise of the rights, of any State under international law with regard to the high seas within that area."[5]

The problem of rights in offshore areas considered by claimants to be under coastal-state jurisdiction was deftly handled in the convention by a device that has become known as the bifocal approach. As several islands whose ownership is not disputed exist within the convention boundary, nonclaimants are able to interpret convention language pertaining to coastal-state rights as applying only to waters around these islands; at the same time, claimant states can read the same text as applying to their Antarctic claims as well as to the islands. This approach enabled signatories to continue to skirt the claims issue and to maintain a delicate balance between the interests of claimant and nonclaimant countries. Negotiation of the living resources regime was facilitated because the ATCPs recognized that management of the exploitation of mobile living resources not only was necessary, given increasing interest in Southern Ocean fishing, but also was in the common interest of all who valued the Antarctic Treaty System.

Mineral resources (with the notable exception of floating icebergs) cannot move through national zones; they are fixed in place. These resources are thus inherently more capable of being exploited by a single national entity if uncontested jurisdiction over them can be established. Hence, the claims issue is more difficult to avoid for fixed mineral resources than it is for the living resources of the Southern Ocean. As the minerals regime negotiations have progressed, it has become clear that the ATCPs intend to sidestep the ultimate resolution of claims once again, but it is equally clear that such issues as title to resources, royalties, and civil and criminal jurisdiction must be addressed in some fashion. To ensure that the interests of both claimants and nonclaimants are satisfied, both creativity and political will are required.

The Need for a New Regime

The need for a minerals regime for Antarctica can be explained in part by the evolution of science and technology and in part by the degree to which the ATCPs came to value the preservation of Antarctica in the early 1960s; however, after more than a quarter century of research, scientists today have a much more accurate understanding of the continent. It is now known that Antarctica's geologic provinces are directly related to those of the surrounding continental land masses, and that Antarctica differs from other continents only in that it is almost completely covered by ice. Scientists have discovered occurrences[6] of many minerals that, *if found in sufficient quantities in more accessible parts of the world,* would be economically exploitable. Some evidence exists that Antarctica contains oil and gas, although no commercially oriented drilling has yet been done, and it is unknown whether any large hydrocarbon deposits exist there.

The means to exploit resources have also improved significantly since the Antarctic Treaty was ratified. This is particularly true with technology for developing offshore oil—the resource that would probably be of most interest were it found in sufficient quantities in Antarctica. Oil companies are venturing into ever-deeper water in the search for new prospects and into seasonally ice-covered areas of Arctic and sub-Arctic regions.[7] Devices such as Exxon's Concrete Island Drilling Structure, man-made floating and grounded ice islands, and artificial islands made of sand and gravel have been designed specifically to withstand the rigors of offshore oil exploration in ice-covered frontier areas. Although Antarctica is a more difficult environment for exploration and development of oil resources than anywhere explored to date, it is fair to say that discovery of deposits large enough to be economically exploitable would stimulate the development of the required production technology—if legal and political constraints to development were removed.

Better understanding of the geology of Antarctica and improved exploration technology have increased the probability that if significant resources exist in Antarctica, they will be found. Although even significant deposits of nonliving resources are unlikely to be exploited in the near future, the possibility that they may someday be exploited is of concern to the ATCPs. Politics plays an important role. The Antarctic Treaty was originally crafted as a delicate balance between the interests of claimant and nonclaimant signatories. Over the years claimants and nonclaimants alike have developed a strong stake in the preservation of the treaty, which, despite its shortcomings, has enabled unhindered scientific research and has kept Antarctica peaceful and demilitarized.

ATCPs believe the entire treaty system may be threatened if valuable resources are discovered before an effective regime is in force. For example, although treaty parties have many reasons for remaining in the Antarctic Treaty, they are free to withdraw at any time. In the absence of an effective regime, the discovery of a major resource within a claimed sector (e.g., 20 billion barrels of oil "in place" or a concentrated platinum deposit) may give the claimant of that sector sufficient reason to withdraw from the treaty and to attempt to develop the resource by itself. If a claimant were to withdraw for the purpose of resource exploitation, it can be expected that other ATCPs would protest, some because they also have equally valid reasons for staking a claim to the area, others because they may already have an overlapping claim, still others because the withdrawing claimant would no longer be subject to the treaty system's environmental and other agreements. Such a withdrawal could signal the beginning of the end for cooperative activities in Antarctica. It is not certain what would then occur, but one possibility is that a would-be developer would have to defend its claim with military forces and/or would have to restrict travel and scientific research within its territory, hence defeating the peaceful purposes of the Antarctic Treaty.

If a nonclaimant ATCP were to withdraw from the treaty to exploit a resource, much the same outcome could result. There are no areas of Antarctica that are not either already claimed or subject to future claims or both. Hence, the potential for conflict over resource rights would be great.

Even if the ATCPs conclude a regime regulating minerals exploitation, nonsignatory states could continue to be a problem. Although it is true that few if any countries that have not signed the Antarctic Treaty are technologically advanced enough to exploit a discovery, it is nevertheless equally true that nonsignatories are not bound by the provisions of the Antarctic Treaty and would not be bound by a minerals regime they had not signed.

National Interests at Stake in the Negotiations

From the perspective of the ATCPs, certain national interests are at stake in Antarctic affairs in general and the minerals negotiations in particular. A fundamental national interest for states participating in the Antarctic minerals negotiations is preservation and maintenance of the Antarctic Treaty System. It would be an unsettling blow to the national interests of the ATCPs if political stalemate or ideological impediments within the Antarctic minerals negotiations precipitated collapse of the treaty and its family of agreements. Implicit in this realization are the complementary goals of the ATCPs' national interests in the region, which are well served by the Antarctic Treaty. The treaty provides for demilitarization, denuclearization, and peaceful use only of the continent, as well as the freedom of scientific-research-information exchange and cooperation, unannounced on-site inspection, and the obligation to settle disputes peacefully. Clearly, these provisions in the treaty contribute to promoting geopolitical and strategic stability in the region. In so doing, they promote the preeminent national interest articulated in the Preamble of ensuring that the Antarctic region "shall not become the scene or object of international discord." Thus, preservation of the treaty system must be underscored as a fundamental national interest of states involved in the course of the Antarctic minerals negotiations. To the extent that these negotiations contribute to strengthening that system, they enhance those states' national security interests as well.

Many ATCPs, especially those with advanced technology, also wish to preserve economic opportunities in the region. They want to ensure that their commercial interests will be served by fashioning a regime that will guarantee security of tenure and availability of access in the event that minerals exploitation ever occurs in the Antarctic. Not unexpectedly, pursuit of this interest by the more industrialized ATCP states conflicts with perceived national priorities held both by claimant states (i.e., to protect considerations of their national sovereignty) and less-developed ATCPs (i.e., to acquire to new technologies and secure participation in joint venture arrangements).

ATCPs are also concerned about preserving and protecting the Antarctic regional ecosystem from degradation associated with minerals exploitation. The regime must not only regulate minerals exploration and exploitation but also provide for effective policies to safeguard the local environment from pollution and ensure the conservation of resources. The fragile nature of the Antarctic ecosystem was highlighted for ATCP delegations by the persistent efforts of environmental organizations such as Greenpeace International, the Antarctic and Southern Ocean Coalition, the International Institute for Environment and Development, the Environmental Defense Fund, and the Antarctica Project throughout the negotiation process.

Furthermore, each ATCP aims to enhance its own international prestige and standing by participating in these negotiations. The ATCP members are but 20 of the nearly 200 states engaged in international relations today. In effect, they represent the self-proclaimed stewards of the Antarctic region, and as such, their participation in the Antarctic minerals negotiations process carries with it a certain special political status in the eyes of the international community. Although other states are unwilling to concede that the ATCPs have a unilateral legal right to fashion policies for the Antarctic region, the participation of ATCPs in this series of minerals negotiations is viewed as one of prestige and influence in world affairs.[8]

DISCUSSION QUESTIONS

1. *What factors prompted the Antarctic minerals negotiations? Why did these factors require a multilateral solution?*
2. *How did the Antarctic Treaty System affect the timing of the negotiations?*
3. *What was at stake in Antarctica for the ATCPs?*

REACHING AN AGREEMENT

Principles Governing the Negotiations

At the 1981 consultative party meeting in Buenos Aires the ATCPs decided that negotiation of a minerals regime for Antarctica should begin as soon as possible. Recommendation XI-1 is important because it formally sets out the principles to govern the minerals regime negotiations. Paragraph 5 states that:

1. the Consultative Parties should continue to play an active and responsible role in dealing with the question of Antarctic mineral resources;
2. the Antarctic Treaty must be retained in its entirety;
3. protection of the unique Antarctic environment and of its dependent ecosystems should be a basic consideration;
4. the Consultative parties, in dealing with the question of mineral resources in Antarctica, should not prejudice the interests of all mankind in Antarctica;
5. the provisions of Article IV of the Antarctic Treaty should not be affected by the regime. It should ensure that the principles embodied in Article IV are safeguarded in application to the area covered by the Antarctic Treaty.[9]

Moreover, Recommendation XI-1 specified elements that the minerals regime should contain. Among these elements should be the means for assessing the possible impact of mineral resource activities on the Antarctic environment; for determining whether mineral resource activities in specific areas will be acceptable, and for governing the ecological, technological, political, and economic aspects of those activities determined acceptable. Also to be included should be procedures to ensure adherence by states other than the ATCPs, provisions for cooperative arrangements between the regime and other relevant international organizations; provisions to ensure that the special responsibilities of the consultative parties are protected; provisions covering commercial exploration and exploitation; and a definition of the area of application.[10] Recommendation XI-1 was both the culmination of events leading up to the decision to establish a regime and the beginning of the formal process to do so.

Institutions of the Regime

Many alternative regimes have been suggested for governing activities of states in Antarctica. For instance, ATCPs theoretically could work to establish a condominium and thereby jointly assert sovereignty over Antarctica's resources. Or they might decide to establish joint jurisdiction over resources only, leaving sovereignty questions aside but forming a joint venture to exploit common resources. Some nonparties to the treaty have advanced the idea of establishing an international regime for developing Antarctica's resources similar to the regime for exploiting seabed resources described in the Law of the Sea Convention; others have proposed that resource exploitation in Antarctica be forever banned and that a world park be established.[11]

That the regime evolved in the direction it did reflects the importance with which the ATCPs regard the preservation of the Antarctic Treaty, the difficulty of compromising on the claims issue, the belief of the ATCPs that only those with continuing activities in Antarctica should make the important decisions, and the belief that the regime should not be activated until it is necessary to do so. Hence, exploration and development activities will not be allowed in an area unless a decision is made to permit them. The reverse is true of CCAMLR, in which unregulated fishing is permitted unless there is a decision to regulate or stop it.[12]

After ten formal negotiating sessions and numerous informal meetings, a distinctive proposed regime slowly emerged. The regime has three important institutions: a commission; one or more regulatory committees; and a Scientific, Technical, and Environmental Advisory Committee.

The most important function of the commission will be to decide whether to open an area to exploration and development. This decision will be made by consensus, as is the rule for most other important decisions made within the institutions of the Antarctic Treaty System. Other possibilities were a two-thirds majority vote or a simple majority. Clearly, the requirement of a consensus vote to open an area for exploration would make it more difficult for an area to be opened. To assist in making this key decision, the commission is to be provided with technical advice from the advisory committee. At a minimum, membership in the commission will include all the ATCPs; additional membership may include non-ATCP states that sponsor mining activities.

As now established in the new convention, regulatory committees will be constituted for each area opened by the commission. These committees will be responsible for establishing detailed rules governing activities within their areas of jurisdiction. They will also review exploration and development proposals, determine whether rights should be granted, determine what rights to grant, and oversee any mineral operations that take place. Clearly, the regulatory committees will have much responsibility, and it could be in this forum that deals concerning royalties and other rights may be negotiated between claimant members and other interested committee members. Membership in each of the regulatory committees established will consist of both superpowers, the claimant in whose claimed area mineral activities are contemplated, several additional claimants, and additional nonclaimants including one or more developing country ATCPs. The goal is for regulatory committees to consist of a politically balanced subset of ATCPs.[13]

The Process

The structure of the Antarctic minerals regime is the product of an evolutionary process. Although not so formal as the United Nations Law of the Sea negotiations (1973-1982), the Antarctic mineral discussions have tended to be more pragmatic. Involving only a few states, the negotiations operated very informally to enhance flexibility in the diplomatic process. There was no rigid committee structure, nor was there any need for parliamentary procedure. As to formal guidelines for the negotiations, the Antarctic minerals process used the rules of procedures of the Antarctic Treaty consultative meetings. There were no votes taken on issues of either substance or procedure during the negotiating sessions.

To the extent that a formally agreed committee structure existed, a plenary session functioned to open and close each general negotiation session. This plenary session provided an opportunity for delegations to state their national positions on various issues in a broad fashion. Most states refrained from these statements in the latter stages of the negotiations because their views were well known.

Smaller committees called "contact groups" (or "working groups") were set up to examine specific areas of concern. The Legal Group, for instance, considered technical legal issues such as dispute settlement, compliance, amendment, withdrawal, and liability; and the Exploration and Development Group worked to resolve issues affecting filing and approval of exploration applications and submission of management schemes. A less formal group on the confidentiality of data and information considered procedures for public release of minerals-related data and information and basic protection for proprietary data. Two other contact groups were active during early stages of the negotiations—a Prospecting Group and an Environmental Group—but they disbanded when the contentious issues were resolved. In serving as informal mechanisms for negotiating issues, these contact groups produced discussion papers and reports for the chairman's perusal and his ultimate use in revising texts. Working group discussions allowed participants to determine more clearly where delegations stood on issues, and their papers demonstrated where consensus was crystallizing.

The Antarctic minerals negotiating process has depended on the manner in which these interests were perceived and translated by ATCP governments into national policy positions. For example, the negotiating position of the United States on Antarctic minerals issues was derived from a set of instructions drawn up by an interagency task force, the Antarctic Policy Group (APG). Within the APG, debate has taken place over the ways for addressing various policy questions and the most appropriate policy alternatives to be followed. To produce a unified policy best serving U.S. national interests, the Department of State initiated the process by drafting a position paper that embodied agreement on issues by the Legal Adviser's Office, the Bureau of Oceans and International Environmental and Scientific Affairs, and the Economic Bureau. This paper then was circulated to the APG.

The APG served as the source of most members on the national delegation to the Antarctic minerals negotiations and is primarily composed of federal agency representatives having special Antarctic concerns. These include, inter alia, the Departments of State, Interior (especially the U.S. Geological Survey), Energy, Defense, and Commerce (National Oceanic and Atmospheric Administration), as well as the Marine Mammals Commission, Environmental Protection Agency, National Science Foundation, and Arms Control and Disarmament Agency. The APG is advised by the Antarctic Public Advisory Committee (APACE), a group drawn from public international organizations, industry, and the academic community. The APACE meets two or three times each year with the APG and various congressional staff to discuss Antarctic issues and U.S. policies.

In general, the APG task force, after appropriate study, formulates a package of proposals that best represents the national interests of the United States and reflects those particular policies to be sought within the negotiating framework. A set of formal negotiating instructions is derived from these proposed policy objectives. These in turn serve as the preeminent guide for U.S. policy in negotiating various points in the international negotiations. The Antarctic minerals delegation consisted of a public interest representative from the International Institute for Environment and Development, an industry representative from the American Petroleum Institute, and a private technical adviser from the academic community, as well as APG members.

At the international level, members of delegations took into account how much domestic factors affecting the national interest weighed in the situation. For example, interests and policies differed, depending on whether a state is potentially a producer or a consumer of Antarctic minerals. The acceptability of particular negotiating points was determined by a mix of factors, involving political, legal, economic, and environmental considerations. Each state appraised those factors differently, a situation that created opportunities for trade-offs. The Antarctic mineral negotiations have sought to balance national interests in a regulatory regime for minerals and the maintenance of the Antarctic Treaty System with other, more individual, ATCP priorities that advocate privileged rights for claimant nations, demands for special participation in decisionmaking organs, and special rights for developing nations.

The Role of Informal Diplomacy

Informal negotiations outside the formal sessions contributed immensely to the process of reaching an agreement. Whereas major points were broadly clarified in general debate, informal diplomacy during the Antarctic minerals negotiations assumed a salient, even vital, role. Such "corridor diplomacy" facilitated the search for practical solutions through informal encounters among the delegates. In fact, a coffee break was intentionally scheduled midway through both the morning and the afternoon sessions of general plenary discussion so as to enhance opportunities for dialogue. At times, the chairman even changed the timing of the coffee break. This was done not only to dissipate negotiating tensions over a particular issue or to relieve the tedium of a speaker, but also to foster more informal exchange of views among the body delegates or to prolong a constructive exchange.

Informal negotiations tended to be direct and issue specific and usually were not obscured by either the political rhetoric or the ideological undercurrents that often typified the more formal negotiating sessions. It is clear that the consensus and progress attained in the formal sessions stemmed directly from the process of informal diplomacy. This fact may not be overly surprising, given that much of the negotiations were informal in character outside the plenary sessions, as well as between the sessions.

As noted previously, the Antarctic Treaty System has operated through consensus decisionmaking. During the Antarctic minerals negotiations, consequently, the objective of attaining consensus tended to permeate the entire process. Near the close of each main plenary negotiating session, the chairmen of the contact groups provided a "written/oral report" that presented the outcome of those discussions. Although these reports by the chairmen were supposed to reflect consensus, the report's content often explicitly indicated on what points delegations failed to agree. No rebuttal or critique of points raised or views expressed in a group chairman's report occurred at that plenary session. Such debate was characteristically left for the next round of discussions.

The Role of the Chairman

A vital ingredient in the Antarctic minerals negotiating process was the role and personality of the chairman, Ambassador Christopher Beeby of New Zealand. He engaged in considerable personal diplomacy, amounting to a continuous series of personal consultations with the heads of national delegations. This latter group of senior diplomats—sometimes called the Beeby Consultation Group—was extremely important in the negotiating process. Working together as a group allowed them to express directly their governments' policy attitudes toward various negotiating issues. They were also able to engage in direct efforts to secure compromise on contentious points, as facilitated by the chairman. This heads-of-delegations group, in fact, underscored the pivotal role played by the chairman and made it possible for him to promote rapport and mutual trust among the delegates. The cultivation of amiable personal relationships emerged as essential for building consensus.

Chairman Beeby was also responsible for drafting texts of the Antarctic minerals convention. Four "Beeby texts" were drafted between 1983 and 1987. The pattern was as follows: (1) A draft text was produced on the basis of discussions and the sharing of national views. (2) The draft was then read and commented upon by national delegations and the relevant ad hoc contact (working) groups, (3) who subsequently conveyed their views through discussion papers and reports back to the chairman. (4) He then undertook informal consultation to exchange private views in the general negotiating sessions and (5) in various intersessional meetings. The outcome of this process resulted in the production of a new text, which attempted to mirror the evolving consensus. The key to this drafting process was the constant flow of information between the chairman and the eighteen national delegations, mostly on an informal basis.

Critical to the drafting process of the Beeby texts was a series of special intersessional ATCP meetings held in Whangaroa, New Zealand. These private meetings, convened at the invitation of Chairman Beeby three times since 1985, each lasted for about a week and principally involved the heads of ATCP minerals delegations. Although the states attending the Whangaroa meetings have varied, delegates from two states—Belgium and South Africa—never attended.

The Whangaroa meetings provided a common opportunity for ATCP delegation heads to refine issues and seek approaches to solving thorny issues in the mineral negotiations. These sessions furnished a smaller, more informal setting for delegation heads to float ideas with the chairman as well as with each other. The Whangaroa sessions generally accelerated the negotiation process by fostering more intense discussions in a less cumbersome atmosphere. In this manner, they supplied more opportunities for negotiating political accommodations on problematic points than were permitted in the full ATCP mineral negotiations sessions.

The Beeby texts have neither enjoyed nor been accorded the formal status of negotiating instruments during the Antarctic minerals negotiation sessions. Instead, they are characterized as the "chairman's offerings," or "the personal views of the chairman." As a result, these documents function in the obvious capacity as "the basis for negotiation," without being officially acknowledged as a working text. Significantly, although the Beeby drafts have not been accorded legal or formal status as working texts, they have nevertheless served as practical, noncommitted official conference documents. This situation allows for flexibility and openness in the negotiating process. Changes and suggestions can be made without complicating the positions of any particular delegation.

The motivation behind production of the Beeby texts was practical necessity. The Antarctic minerals negotiation process needed a main document on which to focus and concentrate the negotiators' attention. Production of the Beeby drafts as a series supplied a way to determine where in the negotiations facets of consensus lay. In addition, the Beeby drafting process provided the diplomatic vehicle for moving the negotiations forward, to "test the waters," on various negotiating points without having to seek formal agreement on any single provision.

It is important to appreciate that a package-deal situation underpinned the Antarctic minerals negotiations process. The treaty product of these negotiations will either be accepted as is or rejected as a whole. No reservations will be permitted to be registered on substantive provisions. As a result, if a national government is unable to accept a particular provision in the text, that state will have to opt to decline participation as a party.

The package-deal approach carries certain disadvantages. First, it complicates the decisionmaking process because the resolution of each individual issue in the treaty becomes linked to the successful negotiation of other issues. Second, the package-deal approach often generates delays. In general, little need may be felt to press on with negotiations until a problematic question is satisfactorily resolved. In the case of the Antarctic mineral negotiations, this potential problem has largely been overcome by the tendency to put aside key troublesome issues and move on to others. A third liability inherent in the package-deal strategy is that it encourages multiple trade-offs. In attempts to gain bargaining power and bolster political leverage, states may resort to trade-off tactics. Such strategies may introduce new substantive complications and procedural protraction into the negotiating process. However, it is equally true that trade-offs may furnish the means to move a negotiation forward, if indeed the requisite deals can be cut among the relevant parties.

Linkage of contentious issues in the Antarctic minerals negotiations surfaced as a common practice by national delegations. The claimant states asserted sovereign rights to portions of the continent and advocated that special considerations for their "territorial rights" should be represented in the new minerals regime. In contrast, nonclaimant states, who refused to recognize the validity of those claims, were reluctant to recognize the rights because to do so would in effect be tacit acknowledgment of a special place of claimant states in the regime. Further, a schism was evident between the more technologically advanced, developed states and the lesser developed ATCPs. The latter desired to secure preferential privileges and opportunities in light of their less-developed economic condition. The industrialized states—which undoubtedly would have to assume most of the technological investment burden—wanted to circumscribe any concessions of this type. The minerals negotiations were striving to determine the right mix of provisions to accommodate the interests of all parties, without unacceptably encroaching upon the interests of any. As a consequence, during these negotiations, an article-by-article process of revisions occurred, within the framework provided for by the contact groups concerned with those particular issues.

There also existed the problem of changing membership of delegations, which probably led to a more protracted negotiating process. Continuity of personnel is important. When the same people are involved in the same negotiations, the chances often are that the process can be expedited. New members on delegations require training, adjustment, familiarization with the issues, and a general integration into the process. All this is apt to retard the momentum of the negotiations process. Since the minerals negotiations began in 1982, six states—Brazil and India in 1983, the People's Republic of China and Uruguay in 1985, and the former German Democratic Republic and Italy in 1987—became new members of the ATCP group.[14]

It was inevitable that these states' admission into the negotiations would necessarily cause delays in the negotiations process of one sort or another. There also occurred the concomitant situation where original delegations in some cases have repeatedly changed personnel, thereby contributing to the familiarization-with-issues/delay problem. (However, "new blood" on the delegations probably contributed fresh insights and ideas.) The size of delegations also affected the progress of the negotiations. It would appear easier for delegations of two to cut deals with other delegations of two over a problem, as compared with delegations involved in the same exercise having ten or fifteen members on each of their teams.

It is clear that initiation of the minerals negotiations served as the political catalyst for focusing international interest in and attention on Antarctica. The ATCPs' haste to begin conducting minerals negotiations prompted the ensuing United Nations General Assembly debate and the rise of the so-called Malaysia Factor—i.e., the movement led by Malaysia to have the Antarctic region declared part of the "Common Heritage of Mankind." Though not a certainty, this movement might eventually attempt to challenge the lawfulness of the entire Antarctic Treaty regime system.

DISCUSSION QUESTIONS

1. *How effective was the use of "contact groups"?*
2. *What impact did Ambassador Beeby, the chairman, have on the negotiations? What does this reveal about the role of the chair in multilateral negotiations?*
3. *How did informal diplomacy affect the progress of negotiations?*
4. *What were the advantages and disadvantages of the package-deal approach?*

ENDGAME

The negotiations began in 1982 at the Fourth Special Antarctic Treaty Consultative Meeting. In all, ten rounds of talks took place between 1982 and 1988. By the end of the tenth negotiating session, the Antarctic Treaty Consultative Parties had resolved numerous differences. The evolving convention had been painstakingly crafted through intense negotiations in the special session meetings, formal ad hoc working groups, intersessional gatherings, and numerous bilateral consultations. The key figure throughout the negotiations had been the chairman, Christopher Beeby of New Zealand. His personal influence, political credibility, and diplomatic skills had been instrumental in securing agreement on numerous contentious issues among the various actors involved in the negotiating process. Nevertheless, some key differences remained, and unless these could be resolved, no agreement would be possible.

Prior to the eleventh session, the ATCPs realized that the time was fast approaching when they would have to make some difficult compromises. Accordingly, representatives from the now twenty consultative party states engaged in the negotiations agreed that the May-June 1988 session, in Wellington, New Zealand, would be the last session, the one in which the final sticking points would be resolved and a convention adopted. Characterizing the mood of the delegates, one U.S. participant in the negotiations noted that most delegates felt that unless they were able to muster the political will to make some tough decisions soon, the negotiations could drag on for a very long time, becoming a formalized forum in which to agree to disagree. To most, this "outcome" of six years of negotiations was unacceptable.

Many elements of the regime, including the general principles to which all participants would adhere, had largely been settled. However, as the negotiators prepared for the final negotiating session, several critical questions regarding the nature, functions, and procedures of the regime remained unsettled. The most important of these issues related, in one way or another, to differing points of view about Antarctic claims and the rights that accompanied these claims. If the minerals convention were to work at all, it would have to be a carefully crafted balance between the interests of the claimants and those of the nonclaimants. The risk was that a failure to reach agreement on these sticking points could bring about the collapse of the entire negotiation. Negotiators knew that outcome could produce severe strains on the entire Antarctic Treaty System and on the cooperative modus operandi that had earmarked its progressive development since 1959.

The Actors

The actors participating in and affected by the Antarctic minerals negotiations are sharply delineated. By far the most important group of actors is the group that includes the Antarctic Treaty Consultative Parties (ATCPs). These are the governments whose representatives meet regularly every two years to decide policy for Antarctica under the Antarctic Treaty regime. This group, and this group alone, has the power to ratify a new convention and see that it enters into force. By the time of the 1988 negotiating session, twenty states had become ATCPs, including Argentina,

Australia, Belgium, Brazil, Chile, China, East Germany, France, India, Italy, Japan, New Zealand, Norway, Poland, South Africa, the Soviet Union, the United Kingdom, the United States, Uruguay, and West Germany. Sweden and Spain became ATCPs in September 1988, but because they were not consultative parties as of the final session, their votes will not count toward ratification and entry into force of the convention.

Several important divisions exist within the ATCP group. The most fundamental division is between the seven claimant states which assert claims over portions of the continent (Argentina, Australia, Chile, France, New Zealand, Norway, and the United Kingdom) and the other thirteen—the nonclaimants—which do not recognize the legitimacy of those claims. As the final session approached, the claimants, who preferred to retain the right to veto minerals activities in their respective claims, had lingering concerns over revenue sharing, the composition and decisionmaking rules of institutions established by the new regime, the authority over on-site inspections, and details relating to compliance.

Within the nonclaimant group, differences exist between the technologically advanced states and those still developing countries. As leading members of the nonclaimant group, the United States, the Soviet Union, Japan, and West Germany often assumed prominent positions during the mineral negotiations. A principal objective of this group was to ensure security of tenure for their potential miners should mining activities prove feasible on or around the continent. The developing countries, led by India, Brazil, and China, had gained strength during the course of the negotiations. They had steadily improved their bargaining ability and gained influence by adopting a more unified negotiating strategy, undergirded by a common set of objectives. As a group, they were determined to secure guaranteed involvement in activities related to future minerals development. The interests of the developing countries conflicted with the developed states' reluctance to share their technology or to participate in mandatory joint ventures with ATCP developing countries.

In addition to the ATCPs, eighteen other states have acceded to the Antarctic Treaty. Collectively, this group is known as the group of Nonconsultative Parties (NCPs). These governments have a voice but no decisionmaking vote in designing policy for the region. Their role consequently has become primarily one of observers. Included among these states are Austria, Bulgaria, Canada, Cuba, Czechoslovakia, Denmark, Ecuador, Finland, Greece, Hungary, the Democratic Republic of Korea, the Republic of Korea, the Netherlands, Papua New Guinea, Peru, Romania, Spain, and Sweden.

The rest of the international community were essentially outsiders. Certain states such as Malaysia, Antigua and Barbuda, and Sierra Leone had led a movement in the United Nations General Assembly to cut off the negotiations for an Antarctic minerals regime until it could be fashioned into a more universal arrangement. This confrontation in the General Assembly had produced much heat, frustration, and rhetoric, but little in the way of progress toward accommodation or a political solution acceptable to this group.

Key Issues

Prior to the final negotiating session, the chairman circulated a revised draft of the minerals convention. Some progress had been made on various issues at an informal intersessional meeting of fourteen ATCP governments held three months earlier. Still, several critical problems remained before a final treaty could be approved. The most important unresolved issues related to fundamental differences regarding claims. These included:

1. The procedure for voting in the commission: Specifically, there was the question of how far consensus would extend in the new regime. Prodevelopment states opposed consensus, as one state would be able to block minerals activities in the area. Those states with strong environmental concerns, and indeed environmentalists generally, favored consensus, particularly for taking critical, threshold decisions about opening areas. Apparently, highly qualified voting majorities (probably two-thirds or three-fourths) would be required for most commission decisions. Consensus seemed likely for decisions involving an area for minerals activities and for budgetary decisions.
2. Composition of the regulatory committees: These were the limited membership bodies to be created in order to consider applications for licenses and to oversee mineral activities in areas of Antarctica approved for development by the commission. Prior agreement had been reached that both the United States and the Soviet Union would have guaranteed seats on every regulatory committee. Despite agreement, this outcome had provoked severe criticism from developing ATCPs.
3. How potential profits derived from minerals activities in the Antarctic might be apportioned within the regime. Claimant states advocated their rights to receive an automatic share of revenues derived from minerals activities on the continent. They contended that these royalties were essential to the process of internal accommodation in the Antarctic Treaty System. Claimants proposed that such revenues might be generated by their presumed right to tax development activities within their respective sectors. Other justifications for these payments were posed by the claimants in their capacity to set some kind of compensatory fee for relaxing mining rights associated with

permanent sovereignty over natural resources, or in their role as special managers over mineral development activities.

Nonclaimants rejected these suggestions. Even to enter into discussions on such royalty payments matters would give unwarranted credibility to the claimants' assertions that they possessed legitimate claim to valid title. The extenuating legal implications of this situation were such that nonclaimants flatly opposed any consideration of royalties or tax payments to be made to claimant states.

Compromises

There were many reasons to compromise, despite differences, and to find solutions to the remaining problems. One of the motivating factors for the decision to conclude a minerals convention was the increasing outside pressure coming from the United Nations. If the ATCPs were unable to resolve their differences and to present a united front against planning for Antarctica's future in the wider UN forum, the United Nations would get involved and both claimant and nonclaimant interests would inevitably be affected. Moreover, claimants and nonclaimants had cooperated since the 1957-1958 IGY. Cooperation in itself had become one of the most important values to preserve in the Antarctic Treaty System. The Antarctic Treaty and related agreements suited all ATCPs well, and no ATCP wanted to see this system jeopardized.

The claimants to territory in Antarctica—particularly those like Chile, Argentina, and Australia, which all felt very strongly about their claims—had a dilemma. No representative from these countries could ever publicly acknowledge that his country's legal basis for making its claim was weak or that some other countries—notably the United States and the Soviet Union—that had not made claims in the same or other Antarctic areas had as much justification for claims as his country. To do so would weaken his country's negotiating position, leading to a final outcome much less acceptable to his government and therefore much less likely to be ratified by his government. Nevertheless, the claims could be challenged. Though claimant state delegates fully believed in the appropriateness of their countries' claims, they understood well the positions and strength of the nonclaimants and other groups. The group of nonclaimant developing countries (India, Brazil, China, and Uruguay), the newest members of the ATCP club, had some interests in common with other nonclaimants, but they also had some different interests and objectives and saw that world from a much different perspective.

In recent years the lesser developed states have emerged as a political force in the ATCP group by virtue of their number—six of seventeen. Consequently, they have advocated their "special" right to involvement in all activities in the proposed regime, something that the more industrialized states have been willing to accommodate only up to a point. Their specific interests include technological assistance for developing countries in joint ventures, should development ever proceed. Other ATCPs prefer more specific selection attributes for joint venture partners, including the financial soundness of an applicant, the extent of technical skill and experience, the adequacy of environmental measures, and international participation generally, without any mandatory participation provisions. Another unresolved concern prior to the final session was developing-country membership on regulatory committees.

The most important of the remaining issues the delegates had to resolve when they arrived in Wellington in May were the question of how to deal with any revenues that would be generated by resource exploitation and the question of voting rules for key decisions, such as the decision to open an area for exploration and development. Successful resolution of both unresolved issues depended upon whether the claims issue could again be sidestepped because it was very clear that neither claimants nor nonclaimants would give in on their position.

Many of the claimant states arrived at the meeting hoping to secure a special share of any revenues generated from exploitation. Nonclaimant countries could not be dissuaded from their position that no special privileges should apply. To grant special privileges to any claimant would be to accord implicit recognition that claims were considered valid. In any case, nonclaimants argued, most of the revenues, if indeed any were generated, should be used to run the institutions of the minerals convention. Whereupon the claimant states modified their initial position and called for a special share of the surplus revenues over and above the costs of running the institutions. Nonclaimant states objected to this position as well, and for the same reasons. They also pointed out that running the current institutions of the Antarctic Treaty System had already cost a considerable amount of money and that therefore surplus revenues might well be applied to defraying past costs—in which case nothing would likely be left for any special shares to claimants. They also convinced claimants that a special share of revenues generated in one area might turn out to be a special share of nothing. To divide revenues more equally could mean an opportunity to share in the benefits from other areas and to use them for Antarctica as a whole.

Nevertheless, the claimant countries continued to press the issue. They finally accepted that if any surplus revenues were generated by resource development activities, the commission would decide, on a case-by-case basis, what to do with them. On only one small point were the claimant states victorious—the essentially face-saving decision that any surplus revenues should be applied to the parties "most directly affected" by the development, i.e., the relevant claimant states, among others.

On the issue of voting rules, the United States among other countries, hoped the institutions of the regime could avoid making all key decisions by consensus. Consensus decisionmaking would mean that a key claimant state would have effective power to block any exploration and development in its claimed area it did not like and/or for which it had been allocated some type of special benefit. Others noted that consensus decisionmaking had always served the ATCPs well in the past, and that on the very important threshold decision of whether to open an area for development, consensus should be the rule. The United States and others conceded the merit of this argument. However, the nonclaimant countries insisted that if the decision to open an area for exploration and development were to be made by consensus, some other decisions, both in the commission and in the regulatory committees, should be made by less than consensus voting. Why? Because consensus voting favors the relevant claimant. If consensus voting is used, it should be used at the earliest possible stage. Once the threshold decision to open an area has been made, nonclaimants argued, the relevant claimant by itself should not be given a second or third opportunity to dominate decisions. To do so would be to give too much weight to the claimant's "special status" as well as play havoc with the need of commercial enterprises to know that once an area has been opened for exploration and possible development, the rules will not change.

Nonclaimants insisted that at key decision points after the first threshold decision, a coalition of states be able to override the desire of a single claimant. Several all-night negotiating sessions among key states had to take place before an agreement was finally reached. Consensus voting for the important decisions of the commission was ultimately accepted, but as part of a package. Another part of the package—a focus of attention in the final session—concerned the composition and voting procedures of the regulatory committees.

Claimant states advocated that because of their special territorial status on the continent, they should receive four guaranteed seats on every regulatory committee. The claimants also desired the right to individually veto any undesirable activities within "their" sectors. Both of these positions were unacceptable to the nonclaimants, who favored a qualified-high-majority system, preferably a two-thirds vote rule. The claimants' position was further challenged by the nonclaimants who refused to consent to any provisions that either implicitly or explicitly acknowledged validity to the claimants' assertions to title on the continent.

Brazil, China, India, and Uruguay advocated a formula that would set balanced representation for seats on regulatory committees between developed and developing states. This position was rejected by the developed states.

Japan, with the support of the Federal Republic of Germany, had proposed that any state undertaking significant prospecting activities within an area opened by a regulatory committee should automatically be included on the committee. If accepted, this proposal would effectively guarantee potential miners' seats on virtually all regulatory committees. In reaction to this suggestion, claimant governments voiced concern that the expanded size of regulatory committees would dilute their influence in decisionmaking.

Claimants and potential nonclaimant miners favored concentration of decisionmaking power in regulatory committees, with only minimal review influence to be exercised by the commission. Opposition to this posture came from the Soviet Union, Poland, and most still-developing states, as well as the NCPs. This latter coalition generally supported the position that primary review and subsequent approval of all significant regulatory committee decisions should be given to the commission.

As part of the package deal, nonclaimants procured the ability to override the objections of a single claimant (or other state) with respect to decisions made in regulatory committees. Hence, the agreed voting procedure for key decisions (e.g., approval of a management scheme) called for only a two-thirds majority of those present and voting. The compromise finally agreed upon was a "chambered" majority. Thus, for key regulatory committee decisions, the seven-member majority of a ten-member committee had to include at least three claimants and four nonclaimants.

It was finally agreed, however, that regulatory committees could have more than ten members if states sponsoring prospecting activities and/or exploration and development activities were not otherwise members of the committee. Provisions were made for commission review of regulatory committee decisions, which the NCPs had wanted, but the commission's role was limited to reviewing decisions. If it found any inconsistencies with the general principles of the convention, it could "request that Regulatory Committee to reconsider its decision" but could not require a change.

How fragile is the compromise convention worked out among the Antarctic Treaty Consultative Parties? When put to the test, will it work? The test will surely come the first time a state requests that an area be considered for exploration and development. An agreement was reached, however tenuous, because, on the one hand, the balance of power among parties was such that no group had an overwhelming advantage and, on the other, interest in common environmental protection and limiting decisionmaking roles to those with active and substantial interests in Antarctica propelled the parties toward compromise.

DISCUSSION QUESTIONS

1. *What impact did the pressure of time have on the various parties?*
2. *What were the major differences between claimants and nonclaimants at this stage of the negotiations?*
3. *What incentives did the main negotiating groups have to compromise?*

NOTES

1. United States House of Representatives, Committee on Science and Technology, Subcommittee on Energy, Research, Development, and Demonstration and the Subcommittee on Energy, Research, Development, and Demonstration (Fossil Fuels), *Polar Energy Resources Potential* (Washington, D.C.: United States Government Printing Office, September 1976), 20.

2. Antarctic Treaty, 12 U.S.T. 794, T.I.A.S. No. 4780, 402 U.N.T.S. 71, Articles I, II, III, and V.

3. Antarctic Treaty, Article IV.

4. David A. Colson, "The United States Position on Antarctica," *Cornell International Law Journal* 19, 2 (Summer 1986), 291-300.

5. Antarctic Treaty, Article VI.

6. An "occurrence" may be nothing more than a trace amount. In general, available data about occurrences are too few to determine the feasibility of economic development.

7. *Oil and Gas Technologies for the Arctic and Deepwater* (Washington, D.C.: United States Congress, Office of Technology Assessment, OTA-0-270, May 1985).

8. Colson, "The United States Position."

9. Recommendation XI-1, paragraph 5.

10. Recommendation XI-1, paragraph 7.

11. W. E. Westermeyer, *The Politics of Mineral Resource Development in Antarctica: Alternative Regimes for the Future* (Boulder: Westview Press, 1984).

12. T. L. Laughlin, "Minerals Regime in Antarctica," Address before the Eleventh Annual Seminar of the Center for Oceans Law and Policy, University of Virginia School of Law, March 26-28, 1987, 6.

13. Christopher C. Joyner, "The Evolving Antarctic Minerals Regime," in Christopher C. Joyner and Sudhir Chopra, eds., *The Antarctic Legal Regime* (The Hague: Martinus Nijhoff, 1987).

14. In September 1988, the two newest members were added to the ATCP group, Sweden and Spain. They were not ATCP members as of the final negotiating session, however, and so are not included among those ATCPs whose votes are necessary to ratify the new convention.

FURTHER READING

Books

Joyner, Christopher C., and Sudhir Chopra, eds. *The Antarctic Legal Regime*. The Hague: Martinus Nijhoff, 1987.
Westermeyer, William E. *The Politics of Mineral Resource Development in Antarctica: Alternative Regimes for the Future*. Boulder: Westview Press, 1984.

Articles

Colson, David A. "The United States Position on Antarctica," *Cornell International Law Journal* 19, 2 (Summer 1986): 291-300.
Joyner, Christopher C., and Ethel R. Theis. "The United States and Antarctica: Rethinking the Interplay of Law and Interests," *Cornell International Law Journal* 20, 1 (Winter 1987): 65-103.

7

NEGOTIATING THE CODE OF CONDUCT FOR TRANSNATIONAL CORPORATIONS

Starting in the 1960s, there was a substantial increase in the direct investment in developing countries by transnational corporations (TNCs). Many of these countries, because they have fragile economies, had a strong desire to establish guidelines that TNCs should observe. This case study is the only one in the volume organized as a simulation exercise. It focuses on the actual conduct of negotiations in the United Nations and on negotiations within the different regional *blocs* for unified positions. The complexities of regional coalition politics and their effect on multilateral negotiations are demonstrated as the different groups attempt to reconcile their aims with global economic realities. The case draws attention to the limits and possibilities of *large-scale* negotiations under UN auspices, and the effect of external events on actions within the organization.

DECIDING TO NEGOTIATE

Since World War II, the world has been transformed by dramatic technological advances in transportation, communication, and information.

This chapter is an edited version of the case study by Thomas G. Weiss and Donald Lu, International Negotiations on the Code of Conduct for Transnational Corporations, *Pew case study no. 202.*

Transnational corporations were among the first to seize the opportunities afforded by the modern age in applying these new methods of acquiring and transferring knowledge to their investment strategies in world markets.

In the 1950s and 1960s, TNCs claimed greater market shares in an increasing number of countries, a trend paralleled by unprecedented growth in national output. TNC growth in the 1970s was even more pronounced. In the five years between 1971 and 1976, the worldwide stock of foreign investment increased by 82 percent, from U.S. $158 billion to U.S. $287 billion.[1] In the early 1970s, TNCs were based in only a handful of countries. The United States, the United Kingdom, and France had been the traditional home countries for transnational enterprises. However, Japan and the Federal Republic of Germany were quickly emerging as strong rivals.

Similarly, the operations of TNCs were concentrated in a very small number of industrialized countries. Four such countries (Canada, the United States, the United Kingdom, and the Federal Republic of Germany) were host to 40 percent of all direct investment stock.[2] In contrast, some 125 developing countries received only 25 percent of direct investment stock, and much of that was further concentrated in the most advanced oil-producing and mineral-rich developing countries.[3]

Interest in the effects TNC activities were having on development peaked in the early and mid-1970s. In the rhetoric of developing countries and many popular analysts, these companies were mere extensions of former colonial exploitation. The rhetoric cited the prior hegemonic intentions of home countries and the inequity in investment distribution as de facto evidence of the lack of benefits from TNC operations.

Developing countries responded with a more assertive posture in their relations with TNCs. Expropriations of TNC and TNC foreign affiliates' operations doubled from the 1960s to the 1970s.[4] Many of these nationalized industries were U.S.- and UK-based petroleum and mining companies. Developing countries also placed restrictions on foreign minority holdings, prevented foreign takeovers, renegotiated existing contractual arrangements (many of which were held over from colonial rule), and established an increasing number of joint ventures with TNCs.

This image was in stark contrast with the view of the industrialized West: the possibility (if not the present reality) of TNCs' contributing to development with transfers of important technologies, the training and employment of nationals, the development of natural resources, and the provision of much-needed capital. The West promoted TNC activities abroad and encouraged the development of an international economic environment that would be attractive to foreign investment. Although within regional groups there existed a range of views, these two images of the role of TNCs in development reflected the basic assumptions brought to the April 1977 meeting of the Intergovernmental Working Group (IWG).

Negotiating the Code of Conduct: A Chronology

July 1972:[5] The United Nations Economic and Social Council (ECOSOC), upon the initiative of Chile, unanimously adopted resolution 1721 (LIII), which requested the secretary-general to appoint a Group of Eminent Persons to study the impact of multinational corporations on the development process and the implications for international relations.

1973-1974: The Group of Eminent Persons held meetings, heard witnesses, and issued a report and recommendations that suggested the creation of a commission to consider, inter alia, the creation of a code of conduct for transnational corporations and the creation of a research center on TNCs within the secretariat.

May 1974: The General Assembly adopted a declaration and a program of action on the "Establishment of a New International Economic Order" (NIEO).

December 1974: ECOSOC established the Intergovernmental Commission on Transnational Corporations as an advisory body and made recommendations as to the functions of the research center.

December 1974: The General Assembly adopted the "Charter of Economic Rights and Duties of States."

March 1975: The first session of the Commission on Transnational Corporations (CTC) was held in New York. The composition of the forty-eight-member commission was based on geographical distribution: twelve members from Africa, eleven from Asia, ten from Latin America, ten from the developed countries of Western Europe, North America, and Oceania, and five from the Socialist countries of Eastern Europe. Members serve for three-year terms and are eligible for successive reelection. In addition, observers participated from trade unions, business interests, regional organizations, and other UN agencies.

This first session was devoted to the development of a preliminary program of projects for itself and the research center. The program included:

1. the creation of a code of conduct;
2. establishment of a comprehensive TNC information system;
3. research on the effects of TNC operations and practices;
4. organization of technical cooperation programs concerning TNCs; and
5. the creation of a definition of TNCs.

November 1975: The Center for Transnational Corporations began operations as a research unit of the UN Secretariat.

March 1976: The CTC held its second session in Lima, Peru. It set forth a long-term work program, which included the appointment of a group of "expert-advisers" to assist the commission and the creation of the IWG to formulate the specific provisions of a code of conduct. Regional blocs had submitted lists of concerns regarding the formulation of a code of conduct.

July 1976: The center published "Issues Involved in the Formulation of the Code of Conduct," which was sent to states in order to assist them in designing their own proposals prior to the first IWG meeting.

August 1976: Governments and nongovernmental organizations were asked to submit their views regarding a TNC code of conduct.

January 1977: The first meeting of the IWG was held in New York. The meeting focused on a "list of major principles and issues to be considered in an outline of a code of conduct" compiled by the chairman in consultation with the center. The group also agreed on the modalities of participation of representatives of trade unions, business, and public interest who would be present at its second session.

April 1977: The second session of the IWG was held in New York. The chairman distributed his remarks regarding an annotated outline of the code. The first substantive discussions about the form and content of a code were begun.

The Political Climate

When the idea of the code was first conceived of in the early 1970s, it was greeted with great enthusiasm by the Third World, buoyed by its new-found political and economic leverage which had been created largely by the success of the Organization of Petroleum Exporting Countries (OPEC). The early evolution of the code paralleled the formulation of the declaration on the "Establishment of a New International Economic Order" and the adoption of the "Charter of Economic Rights and Duties of States." These documents served as two of the most controversial calls by the South to the North to alter the way that international economic benefits were distributed. These developments followed the first OPEC price rise in late 1973 and a seemingly never-ending expansion of direct foreign investment by TNCs. The expanded role of TNCs was accompanied by allegations that they were infringing upon the sovereignty of developing countries.

The purported role of International Telephone and Telegraph (ITT) in Chile, the proliferation of such popular works as *Global Reach*, and the solidarity of the South were very much a part of the atmosphere surrounding the conceptualization of the code. The stage had been set for swift and decisive movement on the new code of conduct for TNCs as part of a comprehensive effort on the part of developing countries to restructure international relations.

The international political and economic events of the mid- and late-1970s complicated discussions and policies relating to TNCs. The economies of industrialized countries had begun to recover, whereas those of many countries in the South stagnated and declined. Moreover, the development process in many developing countries was beginning to suffer the effects of a general reduction in international capital flows. Foreign government funds slowed considerably and were being more carefully rationed. Private bank lending declined. Debt servicing became a major preoccupation for many developing countries that had borrowed heavily during periods of growth in the early 1970s. For TNCs, developing countries were now being seen as "hostile investment climates" because of growing numbers of expropriations and new restrictive regulations and contractual agreements.[6]

Other incentives for foreign investment in developing countries were also significantly reduced. The effective wage differential between large segments of the developing and developed world had been slowly closing. Tariff and nontariff barriers were gradually being lowered as a result of the Tokyo Round of GATT negotiations, thus reducing the incentive for TNCs to produce within the consumer-targeted country to avoid trade barriers. The United States had begun imposing taxes on TNCs based in the United States. Added to the taxes levied by host countries, this created double taxation for U.S.-based TNCs.

During this time, the unified position of the Group of 77 began to change because the interests of some of the code's most ardent supporters were changing. In particular, Mexico, Brazil, Singapore, South Korea, Taiwan, and Hong Kong were finding themselves as new "home countries" for TNCs whose operations were not substantively different from those of TNCs based in the North.[7] Meanwhile, all of Africa and Central America, a large portion of Asia, and even parts of South America struggled to sustain even marginal economic development and certainly had no significant TNCs of their own. These events provide the setting for the negotiation of the IWG in April 1977.

As elsewhere in multilateral development diplomacy, the regional blocs were the cornerstone of organization for the working group. There are a host of subtle difficulties linked to the exact classification of some nations into regional blocs; nevertheless, common notions are perfectly adequate to understand the divisions among countries. The Group of 77 thus consists of virtually all the countries of Asia, Africa, and Latin America; they are also referred to as the "South," "Third World," and "developing countries." The Western Group consists essentially of the country members of the Organization for Economic Cooperation and Development (OECD); they are also referred to as the "West," "industrialized countries," and "developed market economies." The Eastern Group consisted of the countries of Eastern Europe, referred to as the "East," "Socialist countries," and "centrally planned economies." The Western and Eastern groups together constitute the "developed countries" of the "North."

The main clashes in multilateral development diplomacy occur between the West and the South. In spite of its important role in international affairs, the Eastern Group played a minor role in economic bargaining. Its members justified this by disclaiming any responsibility for the existing international economic system and its malfunctioning and injustice. The South could frequently count upon support from the Eastern Group against the West. The South's trade with and aid demands on the North are primarily addressed to the West, not to the East: access to capital, commodity, and technology markets as well as a fairer deal in decision processes in such Western-controlled institutions as the World Bank, the IMF, and the GATT.

The group system functions to allow all perspectives to be brought forth behind closed doors. Then a spokesperson of a group defines a common-denominator position and negotiates it with adversaries or allies. The group system enables large numbers of delegations to distill common positions and articulate them publicly with a single voice.

In the Group of 77, each of the constituent regional groups works out a regional consensus before these are fused into a Group of 77 position. The group system has thus provided a solution to logistical problems confronted by international organizations seeking suitable methods for multilateral development diplomacy with increasingly large and heterogeneous memberships.

The various blocs had major differences on a number of issues relating to the establishment of the code of conduct. Although there was some consensus that the preamble was to be a general statement of the objectives of the code, there was no agreement as to the nature of the problem. Was it to be stated on broad terms as a consequence of the malfunctioning of the global economic system, or more narrowly as a result of the activities of TNCs, especially the mismanagement in their home countries?

A fundamental issue that had to be resolved was the definition of TNCs. It was proposed that the code apply to enterprises, irrespective of their country of origin and ownership, including private, public, or mixed, that had entities in two or more countries, regardless of the legal form and fields of activity of those entities, which operate under a system of decisionmaking centers, in which the entities are so linked by ownership or otherwise. The Western group wanted to include "state-owned" enterprises in this definition.

Respect for national sovereignty and observance of domestic laws, regulations, and administrative practices were important concerns of the Group of 77. They maintained that TNCs must recognize that domestic legal jurisdiction superseded any international legal authority. Many countries in the group also wanted TNCs to recognize that developing countries had permanent sovereignty over their natural resources, whereas the Western

Group was concerned about the role of TNCs in promoting the development and growth of related industries in home countries.

The extent to which TNCs should conform to the developmental objectives and priorities of host countries was another area of concern to both the G-77 and the Western Group. Some countries in the former group felt the code should legally bind TNCs to providing net inflows of financial resources for developing countries, but many countries of the latter group favored a broad interpretation of "contributing to development" and leaving it to TNCs and individual countries to negotiate the precise nature of this contribution.

Both groups wished to explore the effects of TNCs on the sociocultural values and identity of host countries. The G-77 supported a provision that would prevent TNCs from introducing practices that would adversely affect the society and culture of developing countries.

There was general concern that TNCs should respect human rights and fundamental freedoms. Of particular concern to the G-77 countries were the activities of TNCs in countries with racist minority regimes in southern Africa. They wanted TNCs to be prohibited from collaborating with such regimes, and a number of countries supported the imposition of penalties on corporations and companies that did so.

The political activities of TNCs in host countries were a contentious issue. The G-77 countries wanted TNCs to abstain from direct or indirect interference in the internal affairs of host countries. Many TNCs, they alleged, used their economic power to threaten the sovereignty of developing countries by overthrowing governments they did not approve of or by affecting political systems.

The question of ownership and control of TNCs was also to be addressed in negotiations. The extent to which TNCs should promote indigenization of their operations in host countries, especially the recruitment and training of local nationals and their appointment to managerial positions, was an issue on which the different blocs disagreed. Developing countries also wanted the code to encourage TNCs to transfer technology and to aid in the development of indigenous technological methods. They were critical of the fact that TNCs and governments in home countries imposed high prices for imported technology without adapting it to local conditions.

The Group of 77 and the Western Group were also sharply divided on the matter of nationalization and compensation of TNCs. A number of developing countries claimed that it was the inalienable right of a sovereign state to nationalize the property and operations of TNCs operating in its territory. Furthermore, many Western countries maintained that the code should provide for prompt, adequate, and effective compensation that would be nondiscriminatory, rather than a determination on a case-by-case basis.

Developing countries also charged that TNCs regularly withheld pertinent information about their operations, which made it difficult for host countries to supervise and regulate their activities effectively. In view of this, they argued that TNCs should disclose information on their activities, including financial statements, sources and uses of funds, employment practices, transfer pricing policies, and accounting principles, to their employees, the public, and governments in host countries.

The legal nature and scope of the code was another divisive issue. Many countries argued that the code should become a binding international legal instrument. Some viewed it as a series of recommendations to governments and TNCs. Others maintained that it should be established on a voluntary basis, but that individual states should be encouraged to incorporate its provisions into their domestic laws.

Finally, with regard to the implementation of the code, some countries argued that what was needed was intergovernmental cooperation and the creation of international institutional machinery. There were some reservations about this proposal from countries that feared that increasing the existing bureaucracy would lead to inefficiency and hinder the implementation of the code.

REACHING AN AGREEMENT: A SIMULATION

Working Group Negotiations in April 1977. On April 18, 1977, in New York, Sten Niklasson of Sweden, chairman of the Intergovernmental Working Group on a code of conduct for TNCs, convened a historic meeting of national representatives, nongovernmental observers, and expert advisers to formulate an annotated outline to serve as a basis for the UN Code of Conduct for Transnational Corporations. This session, which was held on April 18-22, was particularly intensive because of the impending full commission meeting scheduled for April 25, in which it was hoped that the annotated outline could be approved so that the actual drafting of the code could begin. Represented in those delicate negotiations were six members of the Group of 77, two Western nations, two Eastern nations, two nongovernmental representatives, and one member of the group of expert advisers:

Group of 77

    African Group
      Nigeria
      Tunisia

    Asian Group
      Bangladesh
      India

Latin American Group
Brazil
Venezuela

Western Group
Federal Republic of Germany
United States of America

Eastern Group
Union of Soviet Socialist Republics
Yugoslavia

Non-governmental Group
International Chamber of Commerce
International Confederation of Free Trade Unions

Expert Adviser
Chairman of Federal Association of German Employers (BDA),
Federal Republic of Germany

Procedure. Delegates should spend the prenegotiation time reviewing the issues of the code discussed above, as well as the positions of their respective blocs and those of allies and adversaries. They should also prepare a brief opening statement of about five minutes discussing their general views about the code and its formulation.

The chairman should identify a selection of key issues in order to begin the drafting of the actual outline of the code. The discussion of each major issue will begin with an informal meeting of nations within their regional blocs to discuss strategies, variance in opinions, and the selection of a spokesperson. This will be followed by a formal session to discuss substantive elements of the particular issue. The formal sessions will begin with statements from the bloc spokespersons, which will be followed by other statements from delegates. Finally, participants will meet in regional groups and as a total group to draft the precise language of the outline. Although decisions can be made by formal vote at the discretion of the chairman and the committee, the working group has previously only acted on the consensus of all participants.

ENDGAME?

In a 1977 interview, the chairman of the Intergovernmental Working Group on the Code of Conduct, Sten Niklasson, addressed the question of what the TNC code would require: "Considering the scope of the code and the complexity of the issues involved, however, not only interest, efficiency and constructive attitudes are needed to meet the expectations as far as this work is concerned, but also time."[8]   The 1980s saw his prediction come true. More than a decade has passed since work began on the UN Code of Conduct for Transnational Corporations. Like so many other UN projects, the code has been caught up in the international machinery that created it. Today the UN appears to be further from a completed code than it was when the idea was first introduced in 1972.

The Continuing Working Group Negotiations

The Intergovernmental Working Group (IWG) became the primary forum for discussing the content of the code of conduct. An enormous amount of labor was contributed by national and nongovernmental delegates as well as the staff at the Center for Transnational Corporations in the drafting of the code.

However, the task was not without delays and complications. The April 1977 meeting of the IWG concluded without a finalized annotated outline. In fact, it required two subsequent meetings to agree upon an outline, which was submitted to the full commission in May 1978.

Based on the IWG discussions and consultation with the Center for Transnational Corporations, the chairman submitted a draft of the code to the IWG in late 1978. This draft has served as the basis for debate and discussions until the present day. The commission further refined it in its final sessions. Nevertheless, many of the major issues have remained unresolved. The substantive and semantic disagreements were noted by the time-honored UN tradition of using square brackets to indicate disagreement.

The IWG submitted its final report in 1982 to the commission and was disbanded. The commission then began its own formal negotiations on the remaining outstanding issues of the code. Since 1983, formal negotiations have been held annually. However, they have never been held for longer than two weeks at a time. The meetings of April 1986 and April 1987 each lasted only one day. Though the rhetoric of wanting to finish the code continues, no substantive progress has been made toward a completed code since 1983.

Center for Transnational Corporations Activities

In spite of the lack of an adopted comprehensive code, the Center for Transnational Corporations has played an active role in facilitating communication and education about TNC issues. Over 4,000 officers of host countries have been trained in issues relating to TNCs at workshops organized by the center. The workshops consist of lectures by international experts, simulation exercises, case studies, and panel discussions.

The center also provides advisory services to governments of developing countries in the evaluation and negotiation of specific foreign direct investment and technology projects. The center enlists the support of teams of experts, including economists, lawyers, engineers, financial analysts, and tax specialists, to provide these advisory services.

The center also collects and analyzes information relating to TNCs and their activities. It regularly examines international standards of accounting and reporting, the role of TNCs in South Africa and Namibia, transborder data flows, and environmental and health protection as they relate to TNCs and specific industries and maintains an information system accessible to interested parties.

The Development of Other Codes of Conduct

Within the United Nations system, the World Intellectual Property Organization (WIPO), the United Nations Conference on Trade and Development Organization (UNCTAD), the United Nations Industrial Development Organization (UNIDO), and the International Labor Organization (ILO) all have adopted codes containing important elements of the draft TNC code. Many of these codes, as well as the OECD "Declaration on International Investments and Multinational Enterprises" (1976), attempt to integrate the regulatory aspect with the national treatment provisions that emerged in the debate over the UN code.

The South has itself begun to act: the African and Malagasy Organization, the Andean Common Market, the Organization of American States, and several Caribbean states have considered adopting their own TNC codes. In addition, many host and home countries have entered into bilateral agreements relating to TNC treatment and activities. Bilateral investment treaties have been agreed upon by European home countries and over fifty developing host countries. Many countries, including the United States, have also adopted their own codes of conduct and have been successfully enforcing them.

NOTES

1. United Nations Commission on Transnational Corporations. *Transnational Corporations in World Development: A Re-Examination*, E/C.10/38, (March 20, 1978), 8.

2. *Ibid.*

3. *Ibid.*

4. The comparative statistics for this period are found in the annexes to the World Bank, *World Development Report, 1986* (Oxford: Oxford University Press, 1986).

5. "Background and Activities of the Commission and the Centre on Transnational Corporations," *CTC Reporter* 1, 1 (December 1976), 6.

6. A discussion of the investment climate during this period can be found in Gerald Curzon et al., eds., *The Multinational Enterprise in a Hostile World* (London: Macmillan, 1977).

7. For a discussion of this trend, see: Krisha Kumar, *Multinationals from Developing Countries* (Lexington, Mass.: Lexington Press, 1981); and Tamir Agmon and Charles Kindleberger, eds., *Multinationals from Small Countries* (Cambridge: MIT Press, 1977).

8. "Interview with Sten Niklasson," *CTC Reporter* 1, 3 (December 1977), 8.

FURTHER READING

Feld, Werner. *Multinational Corporations and U.N. Politics*. New York: Pergamon, 1980.

Jones, Charles A. *The North-South Dialogue: A Brief History*. New York: St. Martin's Press, 1983.

Moran, T. *Multinational Corporations and the Politics of Dependence*. Princeton: Princeton University Press, 1974.

Sauvant, K. P., and H. Hasenpflug, eds. *The New International Economic Order: Conflict or Cooperation Between North and South*. Boulder: Westview Press, 1977.

Sauvant, K. P. *The Group of 77*. New York: Oceana, 1981.

ABOUT THE BOOK
AND EDITOR

International negotiations increasingly involve a myriad of state and nonstate actors who approach major issues from a variety of standpoints and work to determine outcomes acceptable to all. Great powers, military allies, business and industry, LDCs, international organizations, and even domestic politics enter into negotiations on complex issues—ranging from defense and national security to environmental protection and Third World development—that now dominate the global agenda.

Abiodun Williams has assembled a collection of case studies that illustrate the variety and dynamism of this complex decisionmaking process. Cases including conflict resolution in Indochina and mining in Antarctica show students the role of contending national objectives, necessary trade-offs, and efforts at coalition building, as well as the influence of personality and persuasion on the outcomes of major negotiations. A case exploring the investment activities of transnational corporations and their impact on developing countries is organized as a simulation exercise that offers students rare insight into negotiations under UN auspices and the impact of regional bloc politics on multilateral diplomacy.

Abiodun Williams is assistant professor of international relations in the School of Foreign Service, Georgetown University. He is the author of numerous publications on international relations.